WHERE ARE YOU, GOD?

HIS PRESENCE IN OUR PAIN

A Biblical Perspective for People in Pain

by David Vestal

Danalyn Publishing

Editor: Blake Atwood (BA Writing Solutions LLC)
Interior Design: Blake Atwood (BA Writing Solutions LLC)
Cover Design: Rupa Limbu (99Designs)
ISBN-13: 978-0692748480
ISBN-10: 0692748482
1. Christian Living 2. Personal Growth 3. Grief 4. Pain
First Edition

"Why do bad things happen to good people? Why does God allow so much hurt in the world? These are tough questions that, at one point in our lives, we all ask.

This book takes a look at the problematic circumstances of life and how God can use them to mold you and direct you into who he wants you to be. It illuminates how to get the most out of trying situations and not become bitter toward people or toward God. I've heard David say time and time again regarding challenges in our lives, 'We can become bitter or we can become better, the choice is up to us.'

"It has been my honor to stand by David for thirty-plus years in marriage. We have faced some difficult times in those years and we have learned some valuable lessons. One thing that we have learned is, there is purpose behind each difficulty. God will shape and mold us to be more like him, if we allow him to.

"Through lessons learned from his own life and lessons he's learned through the lives of others, David helps us discover the underlying reasons you face challenges in your life. David takes us on a journey into the darkest streets of Dallas. You will get a glimpse into the life of prostitution and drug dealers as seen by a Dallas police officer and learn to look beyond the trying issues of life and look deep into God's purpose. I am confident that once you begin reading the stories within this book, you will not be able to put it down!"

Dana Vestal

"While, it is true that suffering is inevitable, misery is optional. David gives a fresh approach to seeing God's purpose in suffering. I was really blessed by his perspective."

Pastor Warren Samuels
President NEXT Worldwide

"*Where Are You, God?* is a brilliant combination of inspirational and encouraging stories for anyone going through painful times in their life. David shares powerful, modern-day and biblical stories that give the reader a hope, comfort, and encouragement unlike anything I have read before."

John Finch
The Father Effect

"David is my brother and dear friend ... I love him. Though I would not wish it upon anyone, pain stretches us ... sometimes very hard. But, if we learn to embrace pain, as did the apostle Paul, nothing is wasted! Nothing! God will redeem it for His Glory! That's what David is letting God do."

Tony Elenburg
Recording Artist & Worship Pastor, Lighthouse Christian Fellowship
President & CEO Elenburg Creative Group, Rio Vida Music

"This book is easy to read, difficult to put down, and impossible to forget. *Where Are You, God?* is a question that we all have sooner or later. If you've ever asked that question, or know anyone who has, then this book is for you!"

Joe Martin, Jr.
Founding Pastor & Senior Leader, C3 Trinity Church

"David's book gives a candid yet hope-filled perspective of navigating the pain and disappointments of life. I've been so encouraged by his insights. This is a must-read for anyone trying to understand God's role when things just don't make sense. *Where Are You, God?* gives a hope-filled yet real-life look at God's heart for us even when dealing with the unimaginable. I hope you'll be uplifted and encouraged by this candid and creative read."

Jonathan Shibley
President Global Advance

"Refreshing! David has captured the essence of God's presence in the midst of difficult times. It is a privilege to 'proclaim' a gospel message like this from the pulpit. But what happens when the sermon the 'proclaimer' shares requires him to walk out the essence of the truth he preaches? Captivating stories—loads of biblical evidence—David has captured deep truth."

Tim Chapman
President Cross Generational Ministries

"I have known David for over twenty years and I highly recommend him and his book. *Where Are You, God?* gives personal stories and Bible accounts that encourage us to not waste our pain. Everyone experiences pain—it is unavoidable in this life—but pain is not our enemy. If you are going through pain you will find hope, and if you are not, his insights will help you help others through their pain."

Terry Moore
Founding Pastor & Senior Leader, Sojourn Church

"Everyone experiences pain and suffering, but how we handle these hardships is what defines us. David offers insight on how to gain strength from our trials and trust in God's plan for our lives. His servant leadership approach provides guidance and a profound perspective regarding both personal and professional relationships."

Marcy Henson MS APRN FNP-C

In this book David Vestal addresses, head on, the question each of us asks when the circumstances of our lives leave us confused, angry, and tempted to give up. You will get practical advice to help you navigate your circumstances with 'faith' in God's loving care realizing that God will use the pain and trial for his good purpose in our lives. I recommend this book to every person facing a dilemma and wondering, 'Where is God?'"

Tom Lane
Dallas Campus Pastor/Lead Executive Sr Pastor
Gateway Church

CONTENTS

Dedication

I began writing this book over four years ago as God was teaching me about pain, not knowing that in the middle of writing it my wife and I would go through the hardest season thus far in our lives. It was on-the-job training I wouldn't wish on anyone.

But I know hard times will come. Disappointments and hurts are always just around the corner. When you have to watch your family hurt, it will challenge you in every area of your faith. During this time, I found myself surrounded by four of the most amazing people on this planet.

I dedicate this book to my partner and best friend, Dana. I love you and can't imagine how I could have ever gotten through this without you by my side.

My daughter Carisa stood by me and never wavered in her faith or commitment to this family. Carisa, I love you and am so proud of the woman that you are.

My daughter Caitlyn has been a light of love and joy to us everyday. She always has an encouraging word and lives her life with the understanding that God is in control. I love you, Caitlyn.

Lastly, when we sat down and told our children what was about to take place, my son Michael, at the young age of twenty, stood up in the living room and said, "Dad, you are the greatest man of God I know and I believe in you. You are the best dad that I could ever have and I'm proud to be a Vestal." Michael, words cannot describe how you blessed us as we stepped out of our comfort zone and into the unknown. That day will always be with us. The words all of you spoke to me over the last two years will not be forgotten.

I love each and every one of you and dedicate this book to you.

ACKNOWLEDGMENTS

Through all of the trials that I have endured over the last three decades, there has been one constant. Thank you to my wife, Dana, for being that constant example of God's unwavering love, grace, encouragement, support, and belief.

She loved me and stood by my side when I was in the ugly trenches of the Dallas Police Department. She held my arms when I grew weary in the pulpit as a Senior Pastor. She has laughed with me, cried with me, fought for me, and has been the best life partner I could have ever wished for. What a privilege it is to be her husband.

Dana is the most unselfish person I have ever met, always putting her dreams and desires second to her family. The words of wisdom that poured out of her during difficult seasons have been straight from the mind of God. Much of the answers and wisdom conveyed in the pages of the book have come from her steadfast relationship with her Savior.

Thank you to so many of our dear friends who have supported us during this book. Many of you have read and edited tirelessly without complaint. If there are still grammatical errors or misspellings, it's not from a lack of trying. Special thanks to Blake Atwood for his hard work and guidance through the process.

INTRODUCTION

I've been shot at, beat up, spit on, cussed out, run over, and stabbed. But I've learned that the physical pain I've endured in my life never hurt as much or lasted as long as the emotional pain all of us, at some point, must endure.

Most of us hope and pray that we will never have to deal with a traumatic event only to have our protective bubbles burst when it rolls into the trials and tribulations of this fallen world. Pain is a part of this life, and the more quickly we can recognize this, the better equipped we can be to get through it. We'll also be a wiser and stronger individual on the other side.

But there's more to pain than just getting through it. In our weakest moments, God wants to show himself strong.
He can use the difficulties in your life to work good when it appears to be hopeless. God can teach you things in battle you could never learn at rest. When you give your broken heart to God, trusting that he sees you even when you don't see him, he will bring light out of darkness and give purpose to your pain. My hope is that the pages in this book will help you experience such redeemed pain and even be prepared to help someone else through a difficult season.

1

The Laugher
and
The Runner

NBA Hall-of-Famer Charles Barkley once said, "There are only five real jobs: a doctor, a fireman, a policeman, a teacher, and a soldier." Though I don't agree with that completely, my dad was a fireman and a soldier, my mom was a teacher, my wife is a teacher, her mother was a nurse, and my daughter is a teacher. So, according to Charles, I come from a family with "real jobs." I guess it's no surprise that I followed suit and spent ten years as a Dallas Police Officer.

I'm often asked, "David how did you go from a policeman to a pastor?" The journey may seem like a strange path, but the two professions are more closely related than you think: typically, no one calls 911 or wants to see their pastor when something good happens.

While both professions are designed to help people, both occupations often see the worst humanity has to offer as well.

During my first six years as a police officer, that's certainly what I saw. On my beat around Harry Hines Boulevard and Northwest Highway during the 80s, my calls resounded with drugs, prostitution, theft, and murder. I could tell you hundreds of stories of both the good and the bad of what I experienced, but the stories of two otherwise innocent girls are what, I believe, initially started me on an inevitable path toward understanding pain.

———————

The first time I ever saw Robyn, I could tell she didn't fit the profile. None of the girls who worked that street really belonged, but Robyn seemed much more out of place than the others. I'd worked that area for four years by the time Robyn had showed up. I knew these people, from the criminals to the business owners.

When I cuffed Robyn on that particular day so long ago, it wasn't the first time she'd been arrested for prostitution. As we drove to the station, I warned her that five girls just like her had been murdered that year, not too far from where she worked.

She laughed.

It seems that by the time we'd had her booked and her paperwork was complete, she was back on the streets.

Two days later, I received a call over my radio: "Element five-five-three. Take the shooting in progress at two-four-four-eight Park Lane apartment two-three-four. Five-three, we are in route."

Five-five-three is a shooting in progress. It means the caller talking to dispatch is still hearing gunfire. My car was three minutes away from the scene.

Lights on.

Sirens blaring.

Pedal floored.

Neighbors yelling, pointing.

Guns drawn, we ran to the door and kicked it open.

Even in the near darkness, I immediately recognized Robyn's partner, Bonnie. She'd been shot multiple times but was still able to recognize me. "Hurry, David. Robyn's upstairs."

I ran up the stairs and turned left into an open door.

I found Robyn, lifeless.

In that moment, all I could think was, *Why'd you have to laugh, Robyn?*

———————

Robyn's murder had no reason. Some confused teenage boy playing games with his friends had killed her. Witnesses gave us the information we needed to track him down in another city, and we made an arrest that same night. By the time we'd booked him, it was three in the morning. On that drive home, I turned off the radio. I needed silence after a night like that. And I always tried to clear my head of the day's work so it wouldn't follow me home.

As the lights of every Dallas skyscraper receded from my rearview mirror, I thought: *What do I really know about Robyn's life?*

She was truly frightened the first time we arrested her. And she talked to us a lot more in those early days. She told us that she'd run away from home to escape abuse, but she got arrested and placed into a halfway home. Then she ran away from there too, because one of the workers had tried to assault her. Poor kid couldn't catch a break.

I didn't want to keep thinking about Robyn's hard,

brief life, but God had some work to do in me, and it required facing some hard truths about my own culpability in what had just happened that night.

After she ran away from the halfway home, she met a guy in Dallas who'd promised the world to her. "He said he loved me," she said once. Yeah, he loved you because you could make money for him by pretending to love other guys.

With that thought, God punched through my considerable mental and emotional defenses with a gentle yet stinging rebuke: *David, she spent her entire life in pain trying to find out what true love was all about.*

I let that truth settle into me. Her death had left me wondering what I could have done differently.

Should I have done more than just warn her about the dangers all around her?

Did I offer her a way out?

Did I tell her about Jesus?

Did I do enough to help her ease her pain?

In the worst days of her life, in the midst of the pain of not being loved, she had turned to the world and the world let her die.

It always does.

Years later, I'd been promoted to detective in the Special Investigations Bureau Vice Squad. We dealt with cases you'd typically see on every crime-based TV show.

A call came to my desk from a local drugstore: "Sir, we have some, uh, disturbing photos that were dropped off for development. I think someone there needs to see these, quick."

The photos were sent to my office, and it was obvious that the subject of these photos was a teenage girl in trouble. At the time, this wasn't surprising, as we'd received numerous reports of teenage girls being kidnapped and forced into prostitution in Southeast Dallas. And despite being rather hardened to such atrocities since I'd been on the force for eight years by then, my heart hurt for this unknown girl in the photos.

God, you brought the pictures to me. Help me find her.

I passed one photo around to my informants, and in a few days we received a call from someone who knew who she was and, better yet, *where* she was. Along with several other girls, Kimberly was being held captive in a beat-up shack in South Dallas.

At the time, that area was notorious. Dispatch never sent officers in solo. At the very least, two cars each manned with two officers were sent. As soon as we'd located the shack, we asked for and received a signed warrant from a judge to raid the house that night. Seven of us donned all-black and jumped into an unmarked vehicle, then we drove to South Dallas.

Once there, we exited the van and staged ourselves by the front door, just like you've seen on every cop show. After a silent count to three, we busted in the door and were met with what you'd expect in a rundown crack house: smoke everywhere, people laying around in semi-comatose states, and other, more conscious people trying to escape through every window. Plus—and maybe this was just me—an overwhelming feeling of evil.

As the first to enter, I frantically searched for Kimberly from room to room but to no avail. However, we did find eight girls being held against their wills, all malnourished, beaten up, and hollowed out. As I left the house, one of the girls heard me use Kimberly's name.

"Are you looking for Kimberly?"

I turned around and nodded, then escorted her into another room to talk.

"I think she's next door."

"Thank you." I yelled for my partner.

"Rico! You up for hitting the house next door?"

"Uh, our squad's gone. It's just us."

"Well?"

"You know if you're going, I'm going." That's one reason I loved that guy.

I looked at the girl. "Stay here, and stay quiet." I looked at Rico. "Let's go."

We barged into the house next door and found even more girls being held captive. Of course my heart went out to them, but I knew I still had a job to do in locating Kimberly. When we got to the back of the house, I heard someone crying in a closet. I opened the door and saw the girl I'd only known from a photo.

She didn't look anything like Robyn, but she could have been Robyn all over again: young, frightened, out of place, otherwise innocent, taken against her will, suffering.

Rico and I grabbed her and exited through the back door. Outmanned, we left with Kimberly and called in reinforcements to save the other girls.

———

With Kimberly's testimony, we made several arrests the very next day. As she spoke to us, we learned her life story. It was very different from Robyn's, but no less heartbreaking.

Her parents were wealthy, and she was a volleyball star. She was about as typical a Dallas teenage girl could be. But when she was thirteen, her parents had divorced after fifteen years of marriage. Kimberly had chosen to stay with her mom and rarely saw her dad after that. Her mom remarried, but that had made Kimberly feel as if she were receiving even less love and attention than before. Without the necessary support and affection of her parents, she turned to those who would give her what she desired.

Convinced by a friend to run away and meet up with some "cool" boys, the boys persuaded the girls to stay with them for an all-night party. That night turned into two days, then into a week, and then devolved into death threats when Kimberly said she wanted to go home.

When I found Kimberly, she was fifteen, pregnant, and had a number of medical problems from the atrocities she'd been exposed to during her captivity.

Like I said, officers and pastors see the worst of humanity, but maybe that's because we're supposed to be lights in the darkness.

As Robyn's story kept superimposing itself over Kimberly's, I decided that I would do all I could to ensure that Kimberly knew of the deep and abiding love available to her through the life, death, and resurrection of Jesus Christ. I bought her a Bible, some Christian music, and Christian books to read while she recovered at a local halfway home. Before her family could be located, she was transferred to a facility in San Antonio that would better meet her needs. Two weeks after that transfer, I called to check in on her, only to hear that she'd run away.

I thought, *Laughing and running away are just about the same response. Please God, don't let Kimberly's story end like Robyn's.*

———

Praise God for delayed answers. A year later, my phone rang as I was headlong into paperwork.

"This is Detective Vestal. Can I help you?"

"David, this is Kimberly. Do you remember me?"

I paused, but only because I was so surprised.

"Of course, Kimberly! How are you doing?"

"Well, I'm doing great. In fact, I'm going to be baptized at Golden Gate Baptist Church in Dallas, and I want you to be there because it was you that told me about Jesus."

I paused again and covered the receiver with my hand.

DPD detectives shouldn't be heard crying.

Then again, maybe it shouldn't surprise you that I cried. Although I'm a big guy and may have become too hardened by my years on the force, God was—and still is—stronger than any of my defenses.

The immediate results of Kimberly's life change were many. In addition to her finding the only love she truly needed by believing in Jesus, her story became a catalyst for change for thousands more.

Because I'd been so affected by the events that had transpired that night, I wrote and composed a song about Kimberly's long, hard journey from freedom to captivity and back to true freedom in Christ. I'd played guitar for most of my life and had recorded a number of albums, but Kimberly's song vaulted my budding music ministry to a new level. Her song was played on radio stations across the country. I was asked to do radio interviews about the rescue. A new halfway home in Texas for runaway teens was even named "Kimberly's House" as a result of the song. Kim herself wrote a book about her life and has used her testimony as a platform to help other women who feel trapped.

I learned many lessons from the untold hundreds whom I tried to help during my time on the force. But in the painful stories of Robyn and Kimberly, I learned this hard truth: when you turn to the world during your trials and tribulations, you will die—maybe not physically, though that can certainly happen—but spiritually and emotionally. You will look for a quick-fix savior and find nothing but more pain, heartache, and suffering in the end. But when you turn to God, even in your darkest moments, he will set you free, use your circumstances to help others, and give you a Kingdom story. When you can embrace your situation with the arms of God, though it may be difficult to do so, your big trials will produce a big testimony.

Maybe you haven't experienced the wild ups and downs like Kim, but you've suffered. You have areas in your life few people, if any, truly know about. Those unshared sufferings gnaw at your soul, constantly making you reassess your walk with God. So you do what comes naturally to most of us: you seek relief wherever you can find it. The immediate relief of the world can be sinful, or at least lead you toward sin. But the relief doesn't last long before the hurt returns, leaving you empty, confused, and possibly hurting even more.

Several years ago my wife and I stepped away from a church we had started in our home. Starting with twelve great people, the small group grew to over twelve hundred during the course of our thirteen years there. But our last four years were a difficult season for us. We seemed to encounter challenges on every side, then the elders decided to go in another direction. They asked us to resign. I knew that my leadership had not been at its best for the last several years. I'd made some bad decisions, but their choice still shocked us.

I highlight this story to give a fresh perspective on a painful experience we had to work through and how God can move mightily in and through your pain. By itself, losing a job can be difficult. But as a founding pastor of a large church, I lost more than a job.

I lost my income, and my wife lost hers. We lost the place we would typically go to worship while enduring a crisis. We lost friends and the support system a church would otherwise offer. We lost our vision, our reason to stay motivated, and what we did 24/7.

Suddenly, an indescribable and incomprehensible vacuum had sucked the life out of us. My wife and I suffered, cried, held each other, and asked the usual "why" questions every hour of every day during that first month.

At first, we didn't see the hand of God in this transition. To us, it was a bomb that had exploded and turned our entire lives upside-down. We had been in that community for twenty-one years. I'd served as the baseball commissioner and was on the city council. My daughter taught in the same school that she had attended as a first-grader.

Though I have felt rejection many times, nothing in my past had prepared me for that level of loss. Now, my desire is to give you what I wish I would have had: some of the tools God gave us to help us weather the storm and still see God working in and through it.

Sometimes you have to stand under before you can understand.

You may not be able to see God in your current circumstances, but you can have faith that he sees you and he hurts because you're hurting. He will enter into your pain if you'll let him.

Don't laugh when others want to help you. Don't run when tough times happen. Rather, accept God's help and face your pain with the help of the Suffering Servant Himself, Jesus Christ.

2

HERE'S MUD IN YOUR EYE!

While the story of how I lost my church is best left to another book, the immediate result of being removed from the church that had begun in my living room was a deeper, different kind of pain than anything I'd experienced while serving as a Dallas police officer. I didn't know how to handle it, so I turned to the Bible. I talked with my wife. I sought out help in new relationships. What you're reading now is the result of the healing that took place over several years. If even a tenth of what I share might help you weather the inevitable storms of life that threaten to capsize you, my loss will certainly be for your gain.

One of the earliest lessons I learned is that pain isn't what we tend to think it is as Christians. Pain is *not* God's judgment on you. Pain is *not* a direct result of sin in your life (though it sometimes can be). This is made no more apparent than in John 9:1–3: "As he went along, he [Jesus] saw a man blind from birth. His disciples asked him, 'Rabbi, who sinned, this man or his parents, that he was born blind?' 'Neither this man nor his parents sinned,' said Jesus."

Jesus's own disciples thought the man's blindness had been caused by some sin in his life, or, if not that, at least in his parents' lives. But how could this man, *blind since birth*, have even had the time to incur sin resulting in his suffering? Maybe he somehow sinned while still in his mother's womb? That's ludicrous, but that's what the disciples were implying.

Jesus refutes their unfounded notion and reveals the true reason the man was afflicted with blindness: "This happened so that the works of God might be displayed in him" (John 9:3b). Then Jesus spits on the ground, makes a little mud, places the mud on the man's eyes, and tells him to visit a local pool to wash the mud from his eyes. The man does so, and John reports that his sight was healed.

Notably, right before he created the mud, Jesus called himself "the light of the world." Then, he promptly allows actual light to infiltrate the real darkness the blind beggar had experienced for decades.

The man who once was blind but now could see was questioned by the Pharisees following his healing. They couldn't believe he could see. They insisted on maintaining their ancient beliefs: "You were steeped in sin at birth; how dare you lecture us!" (John 9:34). Then they threw him out of the synagogue.

Jesus heard what had happened and sought the man out. Jesus asked him the simple question he asks all who meet him: "Do you believe in the Son of Man?" (John 9:35). Now, remember that the man had never actually seen Jesus prior to this second meeting. The man had received his sight at a local pool and not when he was with Jesus.

So, the man's reply to Jesus's question is genuine: "'Who is he, sir? . . . Tell me so that I may believe in him.' Jesus said, 'You have now seen him; in fact, he is the one speaking with you.' Then the man said, 'Lord, I believe,' and he worshiped him" (John 9:36–38).

By giving sight to a man born blind from birth, Jesus refuted the notion that personal sin equals personal suffering. To get anywhere in rightly understanding how God may use suffering for our good, we must first do away with the long-held, unfounded belief that pain is always and ever a direct result of sin in a person's life.

But we do have to admit that pain is a part of living.

The Problem of Pain

The faster you can accept that pain is a part of this world, the faster you're going to be able to endure suffering while also receiving all that God has planned for you as a result of that pain.

One memorable story comes to mind when I think about coming to grips with the reality of deep pain. In 2013, I had the glad honor to accept an invitation to a roundtable meeting with five well-known men, including Senator Rick Santorum, who was then running for president.

He shared of a striking moment in his own life that occurred during a debate with Rick Perry, the governor of Texas at the time. The moderator asked the men, "What regrets do you have?" Santorum immediately answered, "My daughter Bella."

Though he didn't have the time to share the full

details of the story at the debate, he shared them with our table. The Santorums had been told that their eighth child would be born with a rare disease known as Trisomy 18. They were warned that she would likely live only a few months—if she didn't die before birth.

More than a decade before, the Santorums had already lost a child born twenty weeks premature. Fearful of history repeating itself, Rick had privately decided to resist emotionally attaching himself too quickly and too deeply to Isabella. Because he didn't want to hurt like he'd hurt when they'd lost their son Gabriel, Rick had chosen to protect his heart at the expense of loving his child in need.

But his fear didn't last long. He repented of his selfish choice and entered into his daughter's life wholeheartedly. We didn't have to take his word on that fact either. In April of 2012, a man who could have been president voluntarily suspended his campaign in order to be with his daughter, Bella.

Rick Santorum regretted not allowing himself to love his daughter, but in just hearing the way he spoke about her, I'm sure he doesn't regret his decision to halt his campaign. Though we didn't speak about it at the time, I'm also certain that Senator Santorum and his family have learned much about themselves and about God because of the particular kinds of suffering they've had to endure as a family.

Through pain, God will teach us many lessons if we'll stop complaining long enough to hear them.

Pain is a Sign of Life

When I came upon severe wrecks as a police officer, my first instinct was to look for life. Because seconds matter in situations like those, I needed to find out as quickly as possible whether the people involved in the wreck were alive or not. It was their pain that revealed them to be alive. Their cries and screams, even as anguished and overflowing with immediate shock and suffering as they were, quickly revealed to me that they were still alive— that hope for their physical life still existed. Plus, their pain revealed their need for help.

Now, compare that physical scene to the spiritual battles you may be facing. You may not even call it a spiritual battle, but when you're dealing with how you interact with the people around you, that's always a spiritual battle at its core.

If you've suffered a great tragedy or injustice, much like the Santorums did in the loss of their child, you may fall into the trap of telling yourself, "I'm just not going to feel anymore." After all, if you can numb yourself from the bad, then the hurt won't sting as much, right?

But you can't just numb yourself to those bad feelings. When you choose to not feel, you're also choosing to give up love, joy, laughter, and those other positive feelings. Essentially, you're choosing to die inside. You're opting to live as a hollowed-out person because you don't want to be hurt yet again. If you're hollowed-out, every painful event can only affect you on a surface-level. But every good event feels muted too.

You become a silent sufferer, and no one near you knows you're suffering.

Pain reveals life. This side of heaven, to suffer is to live. But on the other side of suffering, if we could just be patient and humble enough, lie the reasons behind why we've been hurt. And even if those reasons don't fully reveal themselves until after we're gone from this world, the Ultimate Sufferer stands ready to empathize with you.

God can use pain in incredibly beneficial ways if only we'll allow him to move in our lives. Then, after he's transformed your pain, he can use your story to help those fighting the same battles you've just overcome.

In fact, I believe pain is a gift.

The Gift of Pain

When my son Michael was nine years old, he had a bright idea. Michael and his friend Connor were jumping on our trampoline, each guy trying to jump higher than the other. They were likely getting fifteen to twenty feet into the air. Then one of the boys saw our oscillating water sprinkler waving back and forth as if beckoning them to make a bad decision.

They were nine, so they made a bad decision.

It may have been peer pressure, but neither boy has ever taken responsibility for what happened next.

One of the boys placed the sprinkler so its arcing water would wave near the trampoline. The other boy turned the water on full-blast. Now they had a visual goal: who could jump higher than the arc of water? Timing was key too. As the water achieved its zenith, these daredevil geniuses planned to jump *off* of the trampoline, *over* the water line, and land on the ground.

Michael jumped first.

He leapt fifteen feet into the air, grazed the spraying water, and then, realizing he'd just accomplished his goal on his very first try, forgot about sticking the landing.

In fact, he hadn't thought about landing at all.

CRACK!

Michael ran into the house, face full of tears and an arm going in the wrong direction.

"Dad, I think I broke my arm."

I looked at his dangling arm and pained face.

"You know what, son? I think you broke your arm."

I hustled him into the car and we went to the hospital where they fixed his arm. He was pretty quiet when the doctor asked how it had happened.

Though there are many moral lessons that could be taken from this story (and I'm sure Michael heard more than his fair share after we got home from the hospital), I'm reminded of how *useful* pain is in our spiritual lives. I know that's a strange word to use when talking about pain, but it's true.

Had Michael not broken his arm, he would have kept making the same poor, destructive decision over and over. Without pain to signify that something was badly out of order, he would have kept jumping and kept breaking every last bone in his body. The pain prevented him from engaging in further destructive behavior.

We need pain to stop us when we can't—or won't—stop ourselves.

We need to recognize pain as the megaphone C. S. Lewis says it is in *The Problem of Pain*: "God whispers to us in our pleasures, speaks in our consciences, but shouts in our pains. It is his megaphone to rouse a deaf world."

Of course, I hurt for my son when he hurt himself so deeply, but don't you think he learned a hard lesson that day that he'll *never* forget?

In the school of life, pain is a chief professor.

3

HUMAN

GARBAGE

DISPOSER

I walked into my billionaire boss's kitchen and immediately smelled what one of his family members had told me I would: a stench like none other. Pinching my nose, I cautiously approached where I thought the offensive odor had to have been emanating from. As I opened the cabinet drawers beneath the kitchen sink, my olfactory fears were confirmed. I'd found the source.

A pipe had busted, but not a water pipe. Rather, it was a garbage disposal pipe. Consequently, every single piece of half-chewed, semi-serrated food had collected beneath that sink for the last week. Maybe even the last month. The congealed mess of former foodstuffs made it hard to tell. But as chief of security, it was my job, apparently, to clean up that mess.

In that moment, on my hands and knees scraping out the nastiest mess I've ever touched with my bare hands, I thought, *I've had enough. I'm done. God, get me out of here. Get me back onto the force. At least there I was respected.*

I may have even said it out loud.

I'm certain no one else was within a ten-mile radius of that sink then anyway.

Who I Was ...

Ten years prior to that toxically memorable event, I had joined the Dallas Police Department right after my wife and I had gotten married. For my first six years on the force, I trained recruits in one of the most dangerous areas of Dallas. I was subsequently recruited to a violent crime task force, which then led me to working undercover for the last four years of my career on the force.

My undercover job required me to infiltrate and break up organized crime rings. If you've seen *Miami Vice* or *Starsky and Hutch*, it was a bit like that, but with Texas accents. In other words, it was intense y'all. Cases could take anywhere from six months to a year to finish.

I truly enjoyed the work and experienced a

tremendous amount of success in what I was able to accomplish during my time undercover. We seized millions of dollars of assets along with houses, cars, and even some airplanes. Along with a good team, I enjoyed some of the best years of my career as an undercover police officer for the big city of Dallas.

And though I wouldn't have admitted it at the time, I loved it when my friends and family would ask me, "So, Detective Vestal, how many times were you shot at today? Any car chases you want to tell us about? What's the most dangerous situation you've been in in the last week or so?"

Of course, I wouldn't give them an answer, but seeing how they perceived me built up my ego. My career was progressing well and I basked in its glory when I could.

But everything has a cost. It's not easy to go out and play the role of a criminal and then to come home and try to play the role of father and husband. You can't just go outside and roll around in the mud, and then come inside, hug your family, and think they won't get dirty. Most of my partners had already been through, or were in the process of getting, a divorce. So I had a decision to make: would I remain in my successful police career or risk losing my family?

When that question presented itself, there was never a question as to which answer was the right answer. I always wanted to be a good husband and father.

But knowing that answer didn't make the transition any easier. The real question was: what would I do if I wasn't a police officer? In my mind, Detective Vestal was famous, but David was a nobody. Without the badge and gun, who was I?

Fortunately, God had plans for my life, even when I didn't have a clue about what I was going to do next. Unfortunately, those plans sent me into the ego-defeating throes of becoming an actual garbage disposer. (Ironically enough, in hindsight I could argue that I'd always been a garbage disposer of a certain type.)

When I finally understood that my marriage was near its breaking point because of my job, I'd already been working part-time as a bodyguard for that billionaire. They only hired trained Dallas police officers. At the time, officers typically weren't paid enough in order to raise their families, so many of us held these kinds of second jobs. Unfortunately, officers today likely have to do the same thing. However, this second job—even with its future that would have me doing menial tasks I thought beneath me—was a blessing in a billionaire's disguise.

When I told the family I was leaving the force and thus would need to leave my position as their bodyguard, they asked if I wouldn't mind staying on with them as their full-time Chief of Security and home-based bodyguard. At that point in time, I hadn't even considered what I was going to do next to earn income. I simply knew that I needed to quit the force in order to salvage my marriage. So, when they offered me the job, I told them, "I'll think about it and pray about it and in Jesus's name, amen, okay, I'll take the job."

The position seemed like a good fit. I still got to carry my gun and wear very nice suits. I hung out with some of the wealthiest people in the world. I still got to play the role of tough guy, and was still able to perceive myself as someone to be feared and appreciated for his special training. All in all, it didn't seem to have been a bad trade-off—but it didn't take long for me to get a reality check.

Have I told you about that time I cleaned out the broken garbage disposal?

That was actually the final straw in a series of perceived slights to my overinflated ego. Because the job was rather low-key most of the time—bodyguards exercise patience more than they do any of their muscles— the family would ask me to do particular tasks: "Hey, David, while you're waiting for the ninjas to come and attack us, would you mind sweeping out the garage and cleaning out the cat box? Oh, and if you can get around to picking up the leaves in the backyard, that'd be great. Some dog left you a nice pile in the front yard."

I may be embellishing that memory.

But I'm not exaggerating my internal reply to their requests: *Somebody needs to tell these people who I am! I am a lean, mean, crime-fighting machine! Two-hundred pounds of twisted steel and godly appeal! I do not do cat boxes, leaves, and dog sh—!*

I may have been dealing with some pride issues then—and an identity crisis. But hadn't I made the right decision in leaving the force? Why was I having so much trouble in this new position that had essentially allowed me to get my marriage back on track? I knew the job wouldn't last forever, but who was I going to be if I didn't carry a gun or a badge? To say the least, my first year as a billionaire's bodyguard was excruciating and humbling.

And then they asked me to check on that terrible smell in the kitchen.

... to Who I Wanted to Be

After cleaning out that rank mess, I stormed outside, angry with God for placing me in a position I thought far beneath me. "God I am through with this! Get me out of here now. I will do whatever you need me to do, but I'm over this!"

He gently but clearly told me, "David, you're going to be here a little while longer."

Like David said in Psalm 42:6, my soul was downcast within me. I couldn't believe what I was hearing. *A little while longer? What does that mean, God? Don't you see what I just went through?*

Sure, I get the irony now of my whining to the God of the universe, the one who suffered immense loss and pain in Jesus's death and separation from him, and all for our sakes. I hadn't really suffered. Rather, just my ego had suffered. But in that moment, I was still asking myself, *Should I stay and finish the job, or should I go back to the force?* As much as I wanted to, I knew I had to heed God's call on my life.

That temptation to go back to where and who I once was is common to us all. When the Israelites left Egypt, it didn't take much wandering in the desert for them to *beg* to be led back to Egypt *where they were slaves* and likely whipped on a daily basis.

Still today, the comfort of the known past often outweighs the unknown anxieties of the future. We fantasize about the past with a keen and deceptive ability to forget the bad parts. This is why some married people choose to reignite old flames via social media. Unhappy with their current relationship, they think back to "better days," completely forgetting why they didn't stay with that person in the first place. (Why anyone would want to go back to that pimple-faced, peer-pressured period of time is beyond me.) Too many marriages have gone up in flames from such reignited fires.

We were created to move through time in but one direction: forward. Our eyes were designed to look forward, our walk to walk forward, and our ears to listen forward. Our noses and mouths are in the front of our faces. God designed us to move forward.

Yet there I was wanting to go backwards, begging God to take me back to Egypt, a slave to my job on the verge of losing his family.

Still, I hated where I was, but I longed to serve God and be the best husband and father I could be. I hit my knees in that backyard, waste on my hands, dirt all over my expensive suit, and tears rolled down my face. In that moment, I finally gave up fighting against his plan for me. I was a prodigal covered in pig slop admitting he didn't know where to go next.

I said, "God, whatever you're doing in me, do it. I am yours."

I stayed in that job for another year, but something deep within changed during my remaining time there: I began to *look forward* to serving them. I anticipated what they needed and got it done before they asked. I discovered that I really enjoyed serving people. My heart began to turn form my selfishness toward the needs of others.

I was leaving who I'd been and finding who I wanted to be.

Temporary Decisions and Eternal Choices

During that last year, my grandmother passed away. As strong, godly people who had served each other every day of their lives together, she and my grandfather John were icons to me. I was asked to speak at her memorial service, and it was my honor to do so.

A time was set aside during the service for anyone in attendance to voice a remembrance of Grandma Vestal. What took place further molded my idea of who God was making me to be.

"I remember when she came to my house and brought groceries when we didn't have any and my husband was sick."

"I remember when she and John came to our house and shared Jesus with my husband and he accepted the Lord."

"I remember when John showed up at our house with firewood, knowing we had no heat and no wood to get through the winter."

"I remember when they both showed up at the hospital and prayed for my son who was sick, and we remember them coming to the hospital after we lost a baby."

"We didn't have a working car, and she would pick us and the kids up every Sunday and take us to church with them. She took my kids to school every morning for two years when we couldn't drive."

This continued until almost everyone in the room had shared some memory of my grandmother and grandfather. It was their collective testimony, spoken by the people they'd selflessly served during their lifetimes.

On the flight home the day after the memorial service, I recounted their lives as I had known them. My grandfather had worked as a low-level machinist for most of his life. Later, he'd worked as a janitor at a bowling alley. To say his vocational career was dull would be an understatement. But somehow neither he nor my grandmother had been defined by their vocations when their lives were over. Rather, they had been defined by their sacrificial lives.

Quite memorably, my grandfather once told me, "David, there are only two major decisions you have to make in life. One is where you're going to spend eternity and the second is who'll you spend this side of eternity with. The rest are just temporary decisions." It was obvious to me that he'd lived his life under those principles.

I had watched him serve my grandmother as she was confined to a wheelchair, as she lost her mental capacity to understand and relate to people, and as her physical ability to take care of herself significantly decreased. I watched my grandpa serve his wife faithfully for *ten years* despite the fact that she could give him nothing in return—at least anything anyone else would have seen from the outside looking in. He only stopped serving her because God called her home.

After her passing, I assumed it must have been a relief for him to not have to do the difficult, daily chores that had been required of him to care for her. Too curious for my own good, I asked him as delicately as I could, "Are you, well, relieved now, in a way Pop?"

With the kind of patient understanding it seems only godly grandpas have, he said, "David, this is the darkest day of my life. God just called my best friend home."

His words struck deeply into my soul. On that flight, I realized my grandparents had chosen to *not* be defined by their vocations, or their bank accounts, clothes, cars, houses, or neighborhoods. They chose to not be defined by what they could or could not do. Rather, they chose to be defined by the Creator of our identities, by the One who knew us before we lived and would know us long after that. My grandparents defined themselves based on their relationship with their heavenly Father.

My grandmother had been known as a woman of God. My grandfather had been known as a man of God. Their core identities were based on who had adopted them: God the Father. He had chosen them to be in his family, and that was all the identity they needed.

It only took me ten years as a cop, the near-loss of

my marriage and my family, three years as a bodyguard, cleaning up rotting, month-old garbage, and losing my godly grandmother for me to *finally* realize that I wanted to have what they had. I wanted to be defined by my relationship with Christ and my service to others. I desired for others to say about me at my funeral the kinds of things my grandmother's friends had shared at hers.

I didn't want to be a big-city detective or a billionaire bodyguard anymore. I just wanted to be David: loving husband, doting father, sacrificial friend, man of God.

A few days after I stepped off of that plane after arriving back home from my grandmother's funeral, God granted me the peace to move forward. No longer wishing for the days that were, I followed his leading and resigned my position, not entirely sure what was next. But I launched myself into intentionally serving others in ministry. In time, God would open doors for me and my family to serve, help, steward, and care for thousands of lives and hundreds of churches.

Looking back now, I wish I would have learned that single, simple truth much earlier in my life: to be known as a man of God is enough.

4

OUT OF

THE FRYING PAN

Rarely do we change when we see the light. Rather, we change when we feel the heat. As much as it pains me to admit it, we need pain.

Like the good, good Father he is, I'm certain God doesn't relish the moments when his children are in pain. But because of his all-powerful nature, "We know that in all things God works for the good of those who love him, who have been called according to his purpose" (Romans 8:28, NIV).

God is more interested in developing your character than in granting you comfort. We're often more interested in the reverse. We want the comfort of Heaven now minus the sacrifice of pain. But God works for your good, even when the good cannot immediately be found.

It's the heat that changes us before we meet the Light.

And if there were any guys in the Bible who understood how to weather the heat, it was Shadrach, Meshach, and Abed-Nego.

Into the Midst of a Burning Fiery Furnace

I've suffered physical, emotional, and spiritual pain, but burn injuries are some of the most horrific imaginable. Third-degree burns are so injurious that they actually negate the injured person's ability to even feel pain. In other words, a type of physical suffering exists that goes beyond pain.

The three young men we meet in the third chapter of the book of Daniel didn't know this, but they certainly knew the real dangers of fire. As Daniel's friends, Shadrach, Meshach, and Abed-Nego were likely teenagers in 600 B.C. Under the captive reign of King Nebuchadnezzar in Babylon, these four godly men were raised from slaves to provincial overseers after Daniel had successfully interpreted a dream for the King. But as egomaniacal kings are prone to do, Nebuchadnezzar starts believing his own hype:

King Nebuchadnezzar made an image of gold, sixty cubits high and six cubits wide, and set it up on the plain of Dura in the province of Babylon . . . .

Then the herald loudly proclaimed: As soon as you hear the sound of the horn, flute, zither, lyre, harp, pipe and all kinds of music, you must fall down and worship the image of gold that King Nebuchadnezzar has set up. Whoever does not fall down and worship will immediately be thrown into a blazing furnace' (Daniel 3:1,4–6, NKJV).

That presented an obvious problem to our teenagers, all Israelite men who each prayed to God every day. In very quick succession, Nebuchadnezzar has asked these men to break the first two commandments of their faith: "You shall have no other gods before Me" and "You shall not make for yourself a carved image" (Exodus 20:3–4, NKJV). But if they don't follow the king's command, they're left with one alternative: death.

However, Daniel and his friends realize that the only reason they've achieved such prominence and comfort is due to following The King (God) and His Law rather than submitting to a king and his law. So, they willingly choose to suffer rather than give in to an idol-worshipping decree. The first time the music begins to play, these teens hold their ground by not falling to the ground.

Of course, people noticed. Astrologers—who likely hated Daniel since he had interpreted dreams they couldn't—snitched: "There are certain Jews whom you have set over the affairs of the province of Babylon: Shadrach, Meshach, and Abed-Nego; these men, O king, have not paid due regard to you. They do not serve your gods or worship the gold image which you have set up." (Daniel 3:12, NKJV).

This is the point where the boys are slowly but surely thrown out of the frying pan and into the fire.

The king was enraged. "So they brought these men before the king. Nebuchadnezzar spoke, saying to them, Is it true, Shadrach, Meshach, and Abed-Nego, that you do not serve my gods or worship the gold image which I have set up?' (Daniel 3:13–14, NKJV).

I have to imagine that Nebuchadnezzar spoke these words as if personally hurt and offended by the young men's failure to be grateful. Essentially, the King is asking them, "After all I've done for you, you can't do this for me?" Nebuchadnezzar then gives them a second chance, but with a stern warning: "Guys, let's try this again. I'm gonna start the music just for you and give you another chance. If you don't bow down and worship, I *will* throw you in the fire. Are we clear? Are we ready?"

Their reply is one of the best illustrations of how we ought to live our lives as Christians today when faced with challenges to our faith.

> Shadrach, Meshach, and Abed-Nego answered and said to the king, 'O Nebuchadnezzar, we have no need to answer you in this matter. If that is the case, our God whom we serve is able to deliver us from the burning fiery furnace, and He will deliver us from your hand, O king. *But if not,* let it be known to you, O king, that we do not serve your gods, nor will we worship the gold image which you have set up.' (Daniel 3:18, emphasis added).

In the New Revised Vestal Version (NRVV) of the Bible, this is how I hear those men's reply to the King:

Hey, King Nebby—don't get all upset. Our answer isn't going to take long. We honor you, support you, and acknowledge your position as king. We appreciate your authority and all that you've done for us. But we will *never* worship you.

You can throw a fit. You can get angry. You can threaten us. You can scream at us. You can do all that you want. But we worship the King of Kings and we honor *His* law— and Nebby, that ain't you.

He will deliver us. We have faith for this deliverance. We believe He can deliver us. He can do anything and everything He wants to do. Our God will deliver us.

I imagine that this is the point where these three teenage guys took a collective deep breath before pronouncing what they all felt deep within.

But even if He doesn't, we're not going to bow and worship you. Even though we have faith *for* this deliverance, our faith is *in* a higher power than you, and He *will* deliver us.

He may deliver us *this* side of heaven or He may deliver us on the *other side* of heaven, but He *will* deliver us. He will accomplish what He says He's going to accomplish.

So, King, that's all we've got to say to you. We appreciate all you've done for us, but if this is the end of our lives, then it's the end.

Our faith is in God alone—not you.

The NRVV would then say,

And King Nebby turned full red as steam poured from his ears, a conniption fit arising from his innermost being. He stood up from his throne and declared for all to hear, 'How dare you snotty-nosed *boys* challenge my throne. Are you kidding me? After all I've done? Fine. You're done. Toss 'em into the fiery furnace! In fact, crank it to seven times hotter than normal. Let your god save you now.'

Of course, this is a paraphrase of an intense event. In Daniel 3:20, Nebuchadnezzar calls for his "mighty men of valor"—the Navy Seals of their day—to escort the teenagers into the fire. He wants to make a spectacle and an example out of Shadrach, Meshach, and Abed-Nego's refusal to worship him. The mighty men bind the teenagers and throw them into the fire.

That's where this incredible story turns shocking.

Because of the king's boiling rage of anger that resulted in a fire seven times hotter than usual, the mighty men are swallowed up in its flames as they place the boys into the furnace. Then the boys—all still alive—fall down "into the midst of the burning fiery furnace" (Daniel 3:23).

Let's press pause on the recounting of this story and pretend we don't know its outcome. Pretend that you're one of the people witnessing this event when it happened.

After the boys' confident speeches about their God saving them, what would you think after witnessing the deaths of those who threw them into the fire? Wouldn't you rightly assume that the God of Shadrach, Meshach, and Abed-Nego had failed to deliver them? After all, their God didn't extinguish the flames or cause a heavy rain to pour. This is the point when most of the onlookers would have begun heading home, like the last minutes of a blowout basketball game.

But they would have missed one of the most incredible events in history. As King Nebuchadnezzar peered from above into the pit he saw something that he could not explain, and much less comprehend.

> Then King Nebuchadnezzar was astonished; and he rose in haste and spoke, saying to his counselors, "Did we not cast three men bound into the midst of the fire?"
>
> They answered and said to the king, "True, O king."
>
> "Look!" he answered, "I see four men *loose,* walking in the midst of the fire; and they are not hurt, and the form of the fourth is like the Son of God" (Daniel 3:24–25, NKJV, emphasis added).

God did not deliver these boys from the fire because he had a greater purpose in mind: "that the works of God should be revealed" (John 9:3, NKJV). We could pull dozens of lessons from this shocking turn of events, but let's consider three specific issues:

1. God didn't deliver Shadrach, Meshach, and Abed-Nego from the fire, but he was *waiting for them in the fire*. The only reason those three men didn't burn up like the mighty men of valor is because Jesus was already there, protecting them from the effects of the enemy's plan. God may not be delivering you from your painful circumstances, but rest assured that he was there waiting for you *before* you fell into your pit.

2. Shadrach, Meshach, and Abed-Nego were bound and chained from head to toe before they were placed into the furnace. Without a doubt, they were at the lowest point of their lives with seemingly no way to escape. Yet when they came out, their chains were gone and they were set free. God will use the fire of the enemy to set you free from bondage.

3. Shadrach, Meshach, and Abed-Nego were public witnesses to their faith in God. In fact, another young man who likely saw their incredible ordeal would face a similar test of his faith just a few chapters later. Could it be that, when brought face-to-face with a pack of lions, Daniel drew strength and faith

from having watched how God had protected and delivered his friends?

But the ultimate revealing of God's purposes still hadn't occurred. Once Nebuchadnezzar had witnessed that the young men were being protected by that "mysterious" fourth figure, the king spoke incredible words:

> Blessed be the God of Shadrach, Meshach, and Abed-Nego, who sent His Angel and delivered His servants who trusted in Him, and they have frustrated the king's word, and yielded their bodies, that they should not serve nor worship any god except their own God! Therefore I make a decree that any people, nation, or language which speaks anything amiss against the God of Shadrach, Meshach, and Abed-Nego shall be cut in pieces, and their houses shall be made an ash heap; because there is no other God who can deliver like this (Daniel 3:28–29, NKJV).

The one who had just fired them (and then literally fired them) was rehiring them. Not only that, but

Nebuchadnezzar—at least in that moment—recognized his inferiority when it came to comparing gods of deliverance. He decrees that his people must not speak ill of their God.

———————

I *love* this story.

Every time I read it, I get more out of it. But for now, the three lessons that leap from the furnace and into my soul are the facts that Jesus is revealed, that he waits for us in the midst of every trial, and that he will free us if only we'll have unwavering faith in his ability to do so— whether on this side of heaven or not.

First, it's amazing that Jesus reveals himself in this way at this particular point in time. The Son of the Most High God has momentarily abdicated his heavenly throne (as far as we know and as far as his physical manifestation is concerned) to visit these faithful young men in the most demanding test of their lives.

And how can we know that the fourth man is Jesus? Because of Romans 14:11: "Every knee shall bow to Me, And every tongue shall confess to God" (NKJV). In other words, when you're in the presence of the King of Kings, your soul knows what's happening, even if your mind and heart know nothing about God. Just witness King Nebuchadnezzar's reaction to this incredible moment and compare that to his emotions and state of mind before he threw the boys into the furnace.

What may be even more amazing is that you don't see Jesus *before* or *after* the fire. Rather, he was *already there*, waiting for Shadrach, Meshach, and Abed-Nego. I'd like to believe that this means Jesus also waits to greet us in the midst of our most troubling circumstances. He longs to protect us, though we will not always escape every trial unscathed.

But more than that, I believe he longs to *deliver* us.

Remember, the three young men were bound with chains before they were tossed into the fire. Likewise, you may be bound with insecurities, fears, and worries of all kinds, the results of gaping emotional wounds you may have yet to acknowledge. You may be so bound up by these issues that you can't relate well to others, or can't worship in spirit and truth, or even order your thoughts. Jesus longs to free you from those issues, though it may require a trial of a fiery furnace to get you to see your need for him. Remember, the young men were loosed from their chains *while they were still in the fire.*

Rarely do we change when we see the light.

Rather, we change when we feel the heat.

5

GROWING
PAINS

Painful life events force you to become someone else. Whether that person is bitter or hopeful depends on how you endure the pain and seek healing in its aftermath. If you'll allow God to do so, he will use the most painful places of your history to grow you into the man or woman of God he desires you to be for your future.

A painful life event can serve as a defining moment that marks when you began to turn from trusting yourself to trusting in God. Pain *will* grow you, but whether that growth leans forward into the sun or strikes bitter roots more deeply into your past is wholly up to you.

Might I recommend the former?

———

The pastor had heard about Cody's wife passing away. As a rancher in Pomona County, Cody's wife was his whole world. Cody hadn't been at church since her passing, so the pastor decided to pay him a visit. He arrived at the ranch just as the sun was setting and found Cody out back by his fire pit, starring at the flames, a.k.a. Cowboy TV.

Cody looked up. "Hey, Rev. What brings you out here tonight?"

"Oh, I've missed you on Sunday mornings, Cody, and wanted to check on you."

"Well, thank you, Rev, but I'm doin' ok. Still just trying to work through everything. I felt it best not to trouble the townsfolk with my problems. I have my own church service right here by the fire."

"Just you and God together? No need for help?"

As Cody nodded his head in agreement, the pastor took a stick and stirred the coals, red-hot and glowing brightly against the dark sky. As they sat in silence, the pastor took one of the coals and moved it away from the fire to the side of the pit. In no time the coal turned dark and lost its heat and glow. After a few minutes, the coal was black and without fire. The pastor then moved the coal with his stick and pushed it back up against the rest

64

of the pile. In no time the coal came to life and regained its brilliant color and heat.

"Well, Cody, let me know if I can help in anyway. It was good to see you."

As the pastor stood up to leave, Cody reached to shake his hand. "Thank you for the sermon, Rev. I'll see you Sunday."

When pain, suffering, or loss occurs, there's no going under it, over it, or around it. You could run away from it, but the hurt will still be there decades from now, and just as painful as it was from its inception. The only way to seek healing from pain and to grow through the process is to *go through* the grief, walking with God and his family beside you.

Thankfully, God grants us blessings in times of pain.

1. God draws you in closely.

Psalm 34:18 says, "The Lord is close to the brokenhearted, and he saves those whose spirits have been crushed" (NCV). For many of us, God feels like he's a million miles away when we're suffering the throes of pain or grief. But your feelings and reality aren't always—and maybe even seldom—the same.

God is omnipresent. He's everywhere all the time. He's close to you in this very moment, yearning to comfort you if only you'll admit to not having a clue as to what you're doing or what you ought to be doing.

Like a "hen gathers her chicks" (Matthew 23:37), Jesus longs to comfort and protect you, but you must be willing to allow him to so do, and you must trust that that is what's actually happening, even if to your comparably, very limited perspective it doesn't seem like anything's happening.

As God tells us through the prophet Isaiah, "My thoughts are not like your thoughts. Your ways are not like my ways. Just as the heavens are higher than the earth, so are my ways higher than your ways and my thoughts higher than your thoughts" (Isaiah 55:8–9).

Yet, in possibly the most shocking conundrum of Christianity, the unknowable, inscrutable, sovereign God of the universe became the knowable, personable, loving sacrificial lamb.

Jesus's life, death, and resurrection ought to show you how much God cares for you and how he longs to bring you close.

2. God grieves with you.

Isaiah 53:3 prophesied that Jesus would be "a man of sorrows, acquainted with deepest grief" (NLT). If you're a Christian, that fact should come as no surprise to you. If you watched *The Passion*, you likely experienced a visceral reaction to Mel Gibson's portrayal of the bloody and brutal crucifixion of Christ. If you've been in church very long, you may have heard sermons that attempt to elicit the same kind of horrified response that Jesus's actual crucifixion must have had on the few people who witnessed it that terrible day.

Yet we're so often prone to complaining to God, "Do you understand what I'm going through? Do you get how much this hurts? So why aren't you doing anything about it? I thought you loved me?" We forget how deeply Jesus is acquainted with grief. We forget that he's an understanding, suffering God—a wounded healer.

He's not aloof like a parent you may have had.

He's not apathetic like a spouse you may have.

He's not ignorant about your pain like a co-worker may be.

He is deeply empathetic because he knows pain.

Just remember the shortest verse in the Bible: "Jesus

wept" (John 11:35). Even though Jesus knew he was going to raise Lazarus from the dead, he still wept with Mary, Martha, and their friends and family because he knew how deeply Lazarus's passing had hurt them. In other words, he empathized with their suffering because he knew how devastating death really was.

3. God gives you a church family.

As Cody learned, you must also learn how to let others into your grief, and the family of God is a healthy place to grieve. We're meant to grieve in community. I firmly believe that healing can come from healthy groups who know, love, and trust each other, even with the most painful parts of their lives.

Over and over again, the Bible talks about the unity of the Church and how we ought to buoy each other in all seasons of life: "So in Christ we, though many, form one body, and each member belongs to all the others" (Romans 12:5, NIV). Paul goes on to say that we should "Be devoted to each other like a loving family. Excel in showing respect for each other" (Romans 12:10, GW). Then, even more specifically, he encourages us to "Rejoice with those who rejoice; mourn with those who mourn" (Romans 12:15, NIV). And we must also recall Paul's lengthy description of how the body of the Church is like our physical bodies: "If one part suffers, every part suffers with it; if one part is honored, every part rejoices with it" (1 Corinthians 12:26). If we are to truly help one another grieve well, we must encourage our communities to be places where we can both celebrate and mourn with one another.

4. God grows you through grief.

As I've already mentioned multiple times throughout this book, God uses the process of grief to grow you into the person he desires you to be—for your spiritual health, your family, church, and community's wellbeing, and ultimately for his glory. God uses pain to get your attention: "Blows and wounds scrub away evil, and beatings purge the inmost being" (Proverbs 20:30, NIV).

Vinedressers know that grapes, which struggled the most to survive, ultimately make the best wine. It's in the struggle that they—and you—grow stronger. In Jesus's last teaching to his disciples, he says, "I am the Vine and My Father the Vinedresser and you are the branch. Every branch that bears fruit He purges so it will bear more fruit" (John 15:2, NKJV).

Entomologists know not to break open the cocoon of a budding butterfly. Its actually in the fight to free itself that the butterfly's wings become strong enough to fly. Without the struggle, the butterfly will be relegated to being a walking insect and will never reach the soaring heights it was intended to experience.

Likewise, God uses pain to bring good from evil: "And we know that in all things God works for the good of those who love him, who have been called according to his purpose" (Romans 8:28, NIV). God also allows pain to prepare us for eternity: "For our light and momentary troubles are achieving for us an eternal glory that far outweighs them all. So we fix our eyes not on what is seen, but on what is unseen, since what is seen is temporary, but what is unseen is eternal" (2 Corinthians 4:17–18).

But that growth will only occur if you can admit our need for God—and your need for growth.

5. God grants you the hope of heaven.

If you believe in Jesus Christ for salvation, then you have the hope of spending eternity in heaven with God. That forward-facing hope can sustain you through even the darkest times of loss, betrayal, or pain. Just as the author of Hebrews wrote, Jesus endured the cross "for the joy set before him" (Hebrews 12:2, NIV).

Jesus surrendered to the cross and never let his focus be hindered. As they stood him up on the cross, his focus was on people, not pain. Just look at the focus of his words:

- "Father, forgive them for they know not what they are doing"(Luke 23:34, NKJV).

- "When Jesus therefore saw His mother, and the disciple whom He loved standing by, He said to His mother, 'Woman, behold your son!' Then He said to the disciple, 'Behold your mother'" (John 19:26).

- "And Jesus said to him, 'Assuredly, I say to you, today you will be with Me in Paradise'" (Luke 23:43).

Jesus was focused on what his present suffering would produce in the future. The joy that was set before him was you and I.

Likewise, we too can face present pain for the joy of eternity with Christ that has been set before us. Paul makes this an even more direct encouragement in his letter to the Thessalonians: "We don't want you to be ignorant about those who have died. *We don't want you to grieve like other people who have no hope*" (1 Thessalonians 4:13, GW).

People without such hope—and I'm sure you know a few—can fall prey to despair much more easily. After all, if all of their hopes and dreams have been placed upon the shoulders of another person, or a new job, or earning more money, and then that person leaves, or they're fired, or they realize that more money solves nothing, what then? What future hope can they look toward to help sustain them through the loss of something so integral to their identity?

That's yet another reason why, as a Christian, you should never be ashamed to share about the hope that you have.

6. God uses your pain to help others.

Have you ever known a reformed addict? Don't they often seem like the best evangelists for getting clean? They often speak as if there's nothing else as important, especially when they're talking to an addict like they used to be. And the chief weapon they use in order to help turn someone away from ultimately killing themselves is *their own story*.

Harry is a close friend whom I grew up with. When I gave my life to the Lord at twenty-one years old, we parted ways. Harry and I had lived a pretty rambunctious sinful life for the past two years and I couldn't live that life style any longer. It had lost its appeal and I had found someone greater and more fulfilling.

Harry was one of the most charismatic people I'd ever met. People loved to be around him. Everywhere he went, he attracted a crowd. His father was a premier pillar in the Chris Craft Yachts industry. Harry followed in his father's footsteps and became one of the world's top salesmen in the same industry. This life brought him money, power, and great recognition, but it also brought everything *else* the world had to offer. I had done my best to keep in touch and prayed for him often but it had been over 30 years since we really connected.

When drugs and alcohol took its toll, Harry found himself divorced, broke, with no place to live, and his only friends were addictions to drugs and alcohol. He landed in jail with nothing and no one near to help. That crisis and deep pain led him to Jesus.

Just a few short months after this, Harry was released from prison and my Sunday morning church service was one of his first stops. To see Harry in church was shocking to say the least. But to see him on the front row sitting beside me was nothing less than a miracle. Harry wasn't just saved. He was radically saved.

He is still one of the most charismatic people I know and has the ability to talk to addicts like no one else I've known. He can relate to them because he's been where they are. He's able to say, "I was just like you. I walked the same roads you're on now. And if you're not careful, you're going to wind up just like me: OD'ed and almost-dead."

This is redemptive pain, the highest and best use of pain. When you can turn your story into a way to help others going through the same ordeal, you provide what you likely wanted when you were hurting and in need of help: someone who understands exactly what you're experiencing.

God doesn't want you to waste your hurt. Paul makes this clear in 2 Corinthians 1:4: "He comforts us in all our troubles *so that we can comfort others*. When they are troubled, we will be able to give them the same comfort God has given us" (NLT, emphasis added).

The next time you experience pain, consider each of the blessings above that God seeks to grant you, even in the midst of suffering. Sometimes—well, oftentimes—you likely won't see these as blessings when you're enduring a painful life event, but if you'll trust God in the process, even when he doesn't seem near, and believe that he will work "for the good of those who love him," you will eventually witness and experience each of these blessings in your life—and all because you chose to let God grow you through your pain.

6

PRECIOUS SUFFERING

You may or may not know who Tony Elenburg is, but he's one of my favorite musical artists.

You may know Steven Curtis Chapman, though. Steven cites Tony as a driving force in getting him into the music industry. Tony and Steven even wrote a number of songs together, and Tony's songs—both his own and the ones he's co-written—have traveled the world, effectively ministering to millions of people. God has used Tony's particular musical gifts to lead people across the globe toward healing and salvation.

But Tony had to endure a painful childhood before becoming the musical artist, and now pastor, that he is. At an early age, he had a promising path in sports. Even as a young man, anyone with eyes to see could tell that he was well on his way toward becoming a six-foot-four-inch athlete. But then his loving and well-meaning parents made a choice on little Tony's behalf that would reverberate throughout his life.

They had him vaccinated for polio.

Tony was one of the rare cases where he contracted polio from the vaccine. The disease caused his right leg and foot to become stunted and deformed. From then on, he walked with a limp.

I'm sure Tony and his parents were upset with such a drastic turn of events for what should have otherwise been a normal day at the doctor's office. As a parent myself, I would have been furious at the doctors, at myself, and at God. After all, why would God have allowed such a promising athlete to contract a disease that would steal that promise from him?

I'm reminded of Jesus's words to the man born blind: "Neither this man nor his parents sinned, *but that the works of God should be revealed in him*" (John 9:3, NKJV, emphasis added). Even if Tony, his parents, or anyone else did not understood why he had to endure such pain as a child and on into his adult life, God still had a plan. Many years later, Tony artfully spoke about that plan in his song, "Precious Suffering":

If the storm makes me more like him
If the night keeps his light from growing dim
I won't fear though my tears fall like rain
Let the storms come, let the night fall, let the tears rain,

Oh precious suffering
You're an old friend of mine
We share a love so bittersweet
for all the work you've done in me
Let the One who suffered most be glorified
Precious suffering you're a dear old friend of mine

Time will come when we say goodbye
When the Father's will in me is satisfied
May sound strange but I'll be sad to see you go
You taught me more love, brought me more joy
Showed me Jesus

Oh precious suffering
You're an old friend of mine
We share a love so bittersweet
for all the work you've done in me
Let the One who suffered most be glorified
Precious suffering

Oh to know the power of His resurrection
But His all-sufficient grace is sweeter still

Oh precious suffering
You're an old friend of mine
We share a love so bittersweet
for all the work you've done in me
Let the One who suffered most be glorified
Precious suffering you're a dear old friend of mine.

Over time, Tony came to see suffering as "a dear old friend," an incredible description of something that seemingly had taken so much from Tony and takes so much from so many others. But Tony knew that the suffering he'd endured had helped him draw close to "His all-sufficient grace."

If only we could all believe and live like that.

Stop Whining. Start Winning.

Tony understood that God would not allow a grape to be crushed before its time. But what in the world does that mean?

For a grape to turn into its best version of itself, it must suffer a crushing. It must be picked, pummeled, poured out, and allowed to ferment before it transforms into the tasty, valuable wine it was always intended to be. Fine wine is only fine after it has suffered a great ordeal.

If you feel like you're in a season of crushing—maybe someone close to you has betrayed you, or maybe a physical ailment is beating you down—maybe God is allowing you to be crushed so he can pour you out in due time. After all, it's the juice within the crushed grape that brings great joy to those who drink its wine.

Now, God doesn't decide to crush you, but he will take what the Enemy means for evil and turn it into something good for his glory and purposes. Unfortunately, we get no say in who or what will do the crushing.

Just read King David's ordeal as a young man.

The Story of a King-To-Be

David wiped the sweat from his brow as he looked back at the house. *Someone's visiting. Probably not here to see me. Better get back to my chores.*

As the youngest of eight brothers, David seldom if ever received any attention. He'd learned to keep his head low and his eyes on his work. Plus, the fact that he wasn't watched all the time provided him with ample time to practice his guitar and perfect his slingshot abilities, both talents that would help him greatly in the future. Even though he was the youngest, he could take care of himself. Though he was slight of frame, he was strong of mind and spirit.

"DAVID!"

One of his brothers was racing toward him.

"What's up?"

"Come quickly. This preacher guy wants to meet you."

"Me?"

"Yeah, you. I don't get it either."

David laughed. "Let's go then. Can you watch these sheep while I'm gone?"

"Sure, but you'll owe me one."

"Of course, brother."

As David approached the house, he heard his father Jesse say, "Yes, that's him, David, my youngest."

The preacher replied, "He's the one."

David thought, *The one? I haven't done anything*

wrong! How could I be in trouble?

As David entered the house, he saw his other six brothers standing there, all looking at the floor. David nodded at his father, but didn't make eye contact with the preacher. The preacher placed his hand on David's shoulder. "You're not in trouble."

David looked up, hope in his eyes.

"You are a blessed young man with a great future ahead of you. I believe you will be a mighty leader in this land."

David's brothers snickered.

Looking at the brothers, the preacher reiterated, "In fact, you may be the one to lead all of us one day."

David's brothers went silent.

"David, can I pray for you right now?"

"Sure, but I don't understand what's going on?"

"You don't have to right now."

News of David's anointing traveled fast and far until it reached the ears of the king. Still confused about what was really going on, David suddenly found himself walking the length of a very long and ornate room to speak with the king. *Wasn't I just in the field watching my father's sheep a few weeks ago?* He shook his head in amazement.

The king spoke. "I've heard you have many talents, including music. Would you mind playing something for me?"

"I'm sorry, sir. I didn't bring my guitar with me."

The king snapped his fingers and an attendant brought forth the most beautiful guitar David had ever seen. It glistened like gold and its strings were real brass, not the twine he'd been used to.

"Play." It was a gentle command.

Though nervous because of his new audience, David took the guitar and played soothing music, the same he'd always done for his sheep. Fluidly, he moved up and down the guitar's neck. As he played, David saw the king's eyes slowly close and his body relax. *If he goes to sleep, how long am I supposed to play?*

David finished the song. An awkward pause ensued. The king awakened, rose from his chair, then started clapping. His staff quickly followed suit.

David didn't know what to do.

"David, will you stay here another day to play that guitar for me? I suffer from, well, I just suffer some days. Your playing, as you saw, brings me peace."

David was smart enough to know that there was only one way to answer a king. "Yes, sir."

That extra day turned into a few more, and then into a few months, and then into years. In time, David was accepted as part of the king's family. Saul appreciated and encouraged the young man. David had found his place as a son with a father he'd always longed for.

In his prayers at night, David would say, "God, I don't know how you got me here, but thank you."

———————

From the king's family to his staff to the citizens who had business with the king, everyone loved David; especially after David had single-handedly helped his people win a war. In fact, this widespread appreciation was so apparent that the king himself grew jealous of young David's popularity. The man who had brought David into his inner circle was slowly turning against him.

"David, play for me." It was a command.

"Of course, sir."

David had only played a few verses before the king erupted.

"Enough! Stop this noise. Get out!"

"Sir, I don't understand what's going on."

"I said, GET OUT!"

"Sir, this music is what's helped you in the past. Why don't I—"

David was cut short as a spear whizzed by his left ear.

"I'LL PIN YOU TO THE WALL."

Fearful for his life, David fled.

The servants he'd come to know and love warned him to never come back. "The king's gone mad, David. He wants you dead. You're too popular. Don't come back here."

For days on end, David hid in the wilderness, living in caves and dining on wild animals. The king's men hunted him, and David knew that if he was found he'd surely be killed.

Overcome with anguish, David fell to his knees and cried through a prayer: *Why, God? Why is this happening to me? What have I done to deserve this? How will you keep your promise from so long ago when that preacher said I'd lead this land? Why are you allowing this? Where are you in all of this? Do you even care about me anymore, or am I just on my own, just like I felt when I was a boy? Why would you take me from the pasture to the palace only to let me die in the wilderness?*

The Power of Pain

I truly believe that your greatest ministry can come from your deepest pain.

As you likely know, David went on to become King David, the most revered King of ancient Israel. God turned what Satan meant for evil into good. And God used David's suffering to forge his character so that he could rightly rule the nation of Israel in due time. We're even given a glimpse into David's thoughts, feelings, and beliefs through many of the Psalms. His ministry—his rule and reign—was strengthened by his past pain.

Consider my dear friend Fabian from Chiapas, Mexico. As a young man, Fabian enlisted in the Mexican Army. He didn't really believe in God but had married a wonderful young lady who did. He had been home on leave for a few days and was going to catch a train to head back to his post. After saying goodbye to his wife,

Fabian tried to jump onto the train as it pulled away, but his foot slipped and he fell onto the tracks. Before he could get out, the train ran over his right leg, severing it at the kneecap.

Fabian entered into a long ordeal of fighting for his life. He'd lost so much blood that his body was too weak to fight off infection. The prognosis didn't look good. Fabian's wife began going to the steps of a small church in the community, crying out to God every day on behalf of her husband. After several grueling months, miraculously Fabian began to get better.

His recovery baffled the doctors, but Fabian accepted the fact that God had spared his life. It was there in the midst of his pain and in a hospital bed that he met God. When he was finally released, Fabian and his wife joined that little church. After several years of serving there, Fabian became its pastor, and he has watched God work through him to build that little church into Solo Cristo Salva Church, the biggest church in the region, serving thousands of people.

Several years ago we were there with Pastor Fabian, helping to put a roof on his church. While there, he gave me a phrase I will never forget: "Valio La Pena."

That was his way of saying, "It was worth the pain." His greatest ministry came from his deepest pain.

Consider Jesus's suffering. Roman soldiers had perfected the perverse art of inflicting pain. They could make a person suffer for an extended period of time without killing them outright. Sharp objects were tied onto leather strips at the end of their whips so that it would grab flesh and rip the body open. Jesus was whipped until his skin dangled from his back and blood poured out. And that was before they hung him on a cross.

Even then, the Roman soldiers were still smart enough to know how to elongate suffering. They would drive nails through the most sensitive nerves on the wrist. Some men being crucified would die from the shock of such pain. But with only a few nails being driven into the wrists and feet, a man could suffer for hours on end, as Jesus did, without dying.

Coupled with such immense physical pain, Jesus also suffered the pain of deep betrayal. He had been rejected by his own people, those who had shouted, "Crucify him! Crucify him!" He had even been rejected by his closest confidantes. The twelve men who had given up everything for him had suddenly given up on him. At the time of his death, all but one disciple had scattered like scared children. Then, of course, and maybe most deeply distressing to Jesus, he felt the full brunt of God's wrath because of our sin.

I'm convinced that there's no physical or emotional hurt that Jesus didn't feel when he was crucified. But through that greatest pain imaginable came the greatest victory humanity will ever experience.

So What?

As humans, we're inherently selfish. We may not want to admit it, but it's true. Even after reading about Tony Elenburg's enduring limp, the young King David's fear for his life, and Jesus's ultimate suffering, we still wonder, *What does that mean for me and the pain I'm in right now? How does them overcoming their pain help me get past mine?*

I'll answer that question with a question: do you remember what photography required before it went digital? You had to buy film and carefully load it into your camera. Then you'd have to take the negatives into a darkroom, douse them in chemicals, and then allow just enough light to reach them so the negative would turn into a positive. What was once a black-and-white photograph would then be revealed in its full-color glory.

God wants to do the same in your life.

Whether you've been mistreated, betrayed, or hurt, God wants to transform the injustices in your life into something much better. He longs to take your negatives, shine the light of Jesus on them, and turn them into positives.

But you may have to be taken into darkness first.

1 Peter 4:19 says, "If you are suffering in a manner that pleases God, keep on doing what is right, and trust your lives to the God who created you, for he will never fail you" (NLT). Remember that Jesus is on the side of those who suffer injustice. Throughout Scripture, God shows special care for people who were unfairly treated. He is a God of justice. He hears your every cry, sees your pain, and knows your hurts. And while he may have allowed that pain to run its full course, he still has a plan to use it for his glory and your ultimate good.

Unfortunately, there are some painful experiences in life for which you'll never receive a satisfactory answer this side of heaven. But God doesn't owe you an explanation. (Just read the last few chapters of Job if you want an "explanation.") The good news is that you don't need an explanation if you trust that God loves you, that he has a plan for you, and that, ultimately, his justice will prevail throughout all the earth.

So what now?

Welcome the light of God's truth into your darkest and most painful places that he might create a beautiful picture of what his love can accomplish, even in the midst of your suffering. "Trust your lives to the God who created you, for he will never fail you" (1 Peter 4:19, NLT).

Believe what Tony Elenburg came to understand: in the right light, pain really can become a precious suffering.

7

THE SUBTLE DIFFERENCE BETWEEN FALLING AND FLYING

Allowing God to work in your life means you still have work to do yourself. You can't just sit back and say, "OK, God, I'm ready to be done with this pain. Do you mind showing me right now what all that suffering was for?"

If only life could be that easy.

Rather, pain takes you out of your comfort zone—literally and figuratively. In fact, it's probably better to say that pain forcibly flings you far outside of your comfort zone. Whether you're physically, emotionally, mentally, or spiritually suffering, pain has a way of turning you into someone you don't want to be. But there are lessons to learn within that pain, if only you could take a momentary step away from yourself.

Pain provides perspective on the possible.

I've been flying airplanes since I was nineteen years old. I've *never* had the desire to jump out of a perfectly good airplane into the vast empty space between it and the ground below. But I have (crazy) friends who do have that desire and have acted upon it many times.

Because I've never taken that plunge, I assume that one's state of being upon jumping could be summarized in two words: sheer panic. But my skydiving friends tell me differently: "As soon as you jump, the air's resistance buffets you, which allows you to navigate the fall and control the experience." It feels more like flying that it does falling.

For me, seeing beyond pain was much the same. I assumed the worst. My fear of the unknown jaded my perspective on what was possible. Without the security of my job—even the glorified housekeeper bodyguard gig—I felt that I'd be free-falling into nothingness. But after I quit and started talking to God more about what he wanted me to do next, I found new job opportunities. Even better, I found new friends willing to walk with me through that journey, and old friendships continued to prove their mettle as they stayed with me too. Because I'd finally taken that step of faith outside of the plane of my life as it used to be, I actually got to travel the world and minister to people, families, and communities I would never have had the opportunity to meet otherwise. The reality of my life exceeded my expectations. I probably should have jumped sooner—figuratively speaking, of course.

And though I'm no biblical figure, my story and the similar stories of so many others remind me of the great stories of the Bible where God brought someone through pain and fear of an unknown future into something they never could have seen coming. Instead of falling, they found themselves flying.

Joseph was betrayed by his brothers and sold into slavery, yet he essentially became his nation's ruler. Moses murdered a man and was exiled, but later led his people to freedom. The Apostle Paul killed Christians, but after meeting Jesus bowed-face-to-face, he became a central leader in the early church and the author of most of the New Testament—arguably the greatest Christian in history.

In other words, God has always been pushing faithful, trusting people out of planes and into incredible futures. He can do that for you too.

Just as he did for a man named James in the early 1900s.

The Incredible Story of James Jr.

James Jr. was born to Mary and James Sr., a farmer and minister in rural Missouri. Three years after his birth, the family moved to Hamilton, a large town (for the time) of 2,000 people. Consequently, James Jr. received a well-rounded education, both from working on his parents' farm and attending the city's high school.

James Sr. didn't think his son could cut it as a farmer, so he asked a local retail goods shop owner to give his son a job. Sure enough, his father's intuition proved correct and James Jr. quickly became a successful retail salesman.

Due to poor health, James Jr. moved to Colorado, where he bought his own butcher shop, which ultimately failed because he wouldn't provide liquor to a hotel. With his entrepreneurial tail likely tucked between his legs, James accepted another job as a retail sales clerk at the aptly named Golden Rule Store. Its managers were duly impressed by James's work ethic and offered him a position as a manger of a new store in Wyoming. Hungry to prove himself, James agreed and moved again.

He became a one-third partner in the new store in Kemmerer, Wyoming. Of the two-thousand-dollar investment he had to procure for that partnership, he'd borrowed fifteen-hundred from his hometown bank in Hamilton. But the investment paid off and the store became a rousing success. In just five years, James was able to buy out both of his partners. Then he began expanding, first into Utah, and then into Idaho. Ten years later, he had 175 stores earning fourteen million dollars per year.

By the time the Great Depression hit America with the full force of a knockout punch, James owned 1400 stores across the U.S. When the stock market crashed in 1929, he lost more than forty million dollars, or almost all of his wealth.

The pressure of providing for his employees and his family took an immense emotional and physical toll on James's body. After several break downs, he was unable to neither function nor cope with reality and was admitted to a sanitarium. To go from one of the most influential people in the United States to a mentally challenged individual broke and alone was a long and hard fall that came quickly. While in search of emotional and mental stability, he attended a voluntary church service that the sanitarium provided. That day James heard a hymn that would change his life, "God Will Take Care of You":

Be not dismayed whate'er betide,
God will take care of you;
Beneath His wings of love abide,
God will take care of you.

God will take care of you,
Through every day, o'er all the way;
He will take care of you,
God will take care of you.

Through days of toil when heart doth fail,
God will take care of you;
When dangers fierce your path assail,
God will take care of you.

All you may need He will provide,
God will take care of you;
Nothing you ask will be denied,
God will take care of you.

No matter what may be the test,
God will take care of you;
Lean, weary one, upon His breast,
God will take care of you.

After hearing those verses, James believed in Jesus for his salvation. He laid his failures at the feet of Jesus and gave his pain to Jesus. He chose to believe that Jesus would carry him through his storm and that God actually would take care of him.

Through releasing his stress and worries to a God who deeply cared for him, James began to rebuild his business. Instead of fretting over the minutiae of every store, he hired smart, trustworthy people whom he believed could lead his stores and his company well. He focused his time on traveling the country to personally encourage his employees.

On one memorable occasion in 1940, James visited one of his stores in Des Moines, Iowa. He witnessed a clerk clumsily wrapping a package and offered to show him a better way. On that day, lowly salesclerk Sam Walton, the future founder of Wal-Mart, received an unforgettable lesson in leadership from one of the greatest businessmen of the early twentieth century: James Cash Penney.

J.C. Penney suffered the loss of two wives while building his business, and the immense pressure of providing for so many families obviously caused him pain. But after his personal Great Awakening in 1940, James became an author (*Fifty Years with the Golden Rule: A Spiritual Autobiography*) and lecturer who couldn't stop himself from telling others about God's work through his failures and suffering, and how biblical principles could be applied to business.

His favorite piece of encouragement was, essentially, "Serve God's people and let God take care of the rest." Once he leaned into Jesus's everlasting arms and fully realized that God would take care of him, even "through days of toil when heart doth fail," James Jr. realized an internal success of eternal proportions.

What happened with his business—which recorded sales of $18.8 *billion* in 2005—was just secondary.

Agony allows for assessment.

We're more like the disciples than we care to admit. Sometimes—well, most of the time—I'm incredulous at how they respond to Jesus: *You just saw him feed five thousand people, and yet you still doubt?*

But maybe nowhere in the Bible do we echo the disciples more than in what they say when Jesus is asleep as a storm threatens to capsize their boat: "Teacher, do you not care that we are perishing?" (Mark 4:38b, NKJV). If we're honest with ourselves, this is the cry of our hearts when we experience pain: *Don't you care what I'm going through, God? If you did, wouldn't you stop it?*

Sometimes he does, as he did for the disciples on that particular occasion. But sometimes he doesn't stop the storm from raging. Sometimes he allows death to take a loved one. Sometimes he allows the divorce to go through. Sometimes he allows the layoff to happen.

I don't know all of the reasons why these things happen, but I do know that these events are catalytic if we can let them be so, and if we can remember and truly believe that not everything that happens in life is solely about ourselves and our needs, wants, and desires.

Painful events can be catalytic because they can bring about change. Whether that change is positive or negative depends on your ability to properly and healthily assess yourself. For instance, when you're content with your life, how often do you ask yourself, "How could this be better?" After all, when the ship of your life is in equilibrium, why upset it?

But when storms arrive and you fear that your ship might capsize, you know something needs to change immediately. After making whatever adjustments you deem necessary and getting through a tumultuous night, the dark skies part and the sun returns again. In the light of day, you can then assess the damage that's been done—and then consider what needs to be done to repair that damage.

In the moments of my life when I've been deeply hurt, I've been provided with the perspective, time, and space to make better assessments about my past successes and failures: *why did this happen? Why didn't that happen? What could I have handled better? Where did I go right? Where did I go wrong? How is God using this event to transform me into the person he wants me to be?*

This kind of assessment helps to prepare you for the next assignment in your life. God wastes no experiences in our lives. We do.

After Jesus calmed the storm, he rebuked his disciples: "Why are you so fearful? How is it that you have no faith?" (Mark 4:40b, NKJV). For once, let's try *not* to be so much like the disciples. Let's choose to have faith that God knows exactly what he's doing in our lives, even if the storm overtakes us. And, if he sees fit to carry us through the storm, let's pause and consider why he did so. We will always face pain, and we just make it worse—and may suffer from repeating history—if we fail to properly assess ourselves in light of past pain.

Trauma transforms your thinking.

Our tendency as humans is to go with what we know instead of stepping out in faith into a future that God wants to lead us into. After all, it's easier to brood over the past than to lean into the possibilities of the future. For good or ill, we know the past, but the future is fraught with, well, who knows what? Again, I'm reminded of the Israelites wandering in the desert during the Exodus, complaining to Moses that they *wanted to go back to being slaves* because at least they got fed. We act this way far too often as well.

I see this kind of thinking often play out with men I'm mentoring who have lost a job. Because most of the variables within the equation are known, they'll seek out another job that's similar to, if not the exact same as, the job from which they were just fired.

But what if the previous job was just another tool they needed in their professional belt? What if the only purpose of that previous job was to train them for their next assignment? What if they're supposed to do something wholly different? To many men, myself included, that's like asking them to jump out of a plane. But when you lean into God's plan for your life, he may just change your thinking about making such a jump.

Here's how I prepared for my jump: after losing my job, I created a vision board: a visual reminder of what was important to me (my wife and kids), where I'd come from, and where I wanted to be next year and a few years after that. With such visuals, it was easy to see how God had honed my particular skills in helping other people succeed over the last twenty-eight years despite a number of seemingly disconnected job titles.

As a leader of Otis Engineering's Quality Control Division for six years, I learned the impact of excellent work and how my work could affect people all over the world.

As a Dallas Police Officer for ten years, I had mentored recruits, many of whom were just starting their own families. I certainly learned conflict resolution and crisis management while on that job.

As a bodyguard, I learned how to serve and lay down my entitled ego. Following that, I worked with businessmen and their families to help them get through difficulties. I had the glad pleasure to work with some of the best musicians in the United States. I was afforded the opportunity to hone my public speaking skills with a coach as I traveled throughout the U.S. and abroad delivering speeches. In time, all of these apparently separate abilities coalesced into my calling as a pastor.

God hadn't wasted a moment of my life experiences. When I finally chose to trust him more than myself, he gave me a bigger assignment that would ultimately have a greater impact on people. He verified his promise, "You have been faithful with a few things; I will put you in charge of many things. Come and share your master's happiness!" (Matthew 25:21b, NIV).

And even though pain has still visited me on many occasions, I've never been happier than in serving God and knowing that he's patiently formed me through decades for such a time as this.

Allow the trauma you've experienced (or are currently experiencing) to transform your thinking about how God can and will use you. Be faithful with that "few" thing so that God might grant you favor in many more. And be ready to jump when the time is right.

Suffering strengthens your senses.

Pain brings desperation.

Whether it's a negative diagnosis, relational conflict, or the loss of a loved one, pain ushers you to a place of tremendous need. You may think a desperate prayer:

I can't do this on my own.

I can't make this go away.

I need you, God, now more than ever before.

Pain opens your eyes to what really matters, cutting away the superficial, peripheral issues of your life:

The promotion you've been working so hard for.

The new house you've been dreaming about.

That purse or pair of shoes you've been hoping to get this year.

Those last ten pounds you've wanted to get off.

That frustration you've been having with an employee or family member.

These issues all seem to disappear when crisis collides with your life.

The reality is that you're discovering what have always been the *most* important areas of your life. But you're human, and we just seem to forget about those issues and allow them to fade from the center of our purpose.

I have all types of aches and pains in this old body of mine. In my younger days, I treated it more like a jungle gym than God's temple. I once broke my ankle and tore a major tendon on the outside of my foot. After surgery and several days in the hospital, I was *totally* focused on what really mattered.

When could I walk again?

How am I going to work and provide for my family?

The little aches and pains that I'd complained about in a normal day suddenly went away. I was completely focused on my immediate next steps and needed to reset my foundation. When a painful crisis hits, your sense of what's most important comes to the surface.

Lastly, getting through to the other side of suffering seems to enhance your sensitivity. What I mean is that you may start to feel your emotions more deeply. I believe God may allow pain to infiltrate our lives in order to break through our hardened exteriors. Once the shell that's been protecting your heart has been broken by suffering, the numbness you may have once felt gives way to intense emotions.

Of course, venting such strong emotions could be unhealthy if you give into anger, bitterness, or despair.

But when you can learn how to deal with those issues while still allowing yourself to deeply feel all of your emotions, you can start to live as a more in-tune, intact, relationally and emotionally available person than you may have been before the pain invaded and changed your life.

When the facade of, "I'm okay" finally gives way to the truth of, "I'm in pain," you will certainly hurt more than you have hurt in quite some time. Suffering you've endured over the years, even over the decades, may compound itself when you finally allow yourself to feel the full brunt of that pain. But you should also notice an ability to laugh more than you have in a long time, to savor the happy moments in your life, and to simply be aware of the gifts God has given you, even in the midst of suffering and coming to grips with such suffering.

When you can recognize suffering for the teaching agent it is, you can also start to look at the future with a more discerning and hopeful eye. And even when pain greets you with a familiar suddenness in that future, you'll be more capably prepared to handle it than you previously did. Knowing that God can and will use your painful experiences to draw you closer to him and bring you closer to who He wants you to be, you ought to be able to weather future storms with an eye toward the inevitable dawning of a new day.

And nowhere are dawns more glorious than at 12,500 feet, the typical height for a skydive.

Stop falling.

Start flying.

8

BITTER

OR

BETTER?

"Hey, Joe. Do you have a transmission for a '77 Chevy pickup?"

The junkyard owner looked up at the two teenage kids in front of him. "And you two are?"

Billy pointed to himself. "I'm Billy. That's Eric."

Eric nodded.

"What you boys need with that kinda transmission?"

"Eric's pickup's shot. Just need a transmission to get it going."

Eric grunted.

Joe glanced at the pair. "He doesn't say much, does he?"

Neither of the boys replied.

"Huh. I got one out in the yard. Go about a hundred

feet out that door behind you and take a left where you see a path. You should find what you need already out of the truck. Just watch out for Rufus."

"Who's Rufus?" asked Billy.

"Oh, I'm sure he'll introduce himself."

The boys walked out.

As the door slammed, they heard Joe shout out after them, "And don't touch nothin' that ain't what you need!"

As soon as the boys took the left, they saw an old water well.

Eric walked up to its edge and peered into the darkness below. "Wonder how deep this thing is. Billy, toss me that rock over there."

Eric threw the rock into the well, held out his hand to quiet Billy, then turned his left ear to the well.

After a long minute, Billy said, "I didn't hear it hit."

"Me neither."

"Toss me that battery."

Eric repeated the process, but the outcome was still the same: silence.

"Okay. That's weird. What kind of well is this?"

Eric looked around the junkyard for something just a bit larger.

"Billy, look over there, over by where we turned. Is that an engine block? Think that'll fit in the well?"

"Yeah, but . . ."

"But what?"

"Ol' Joe said we shouldn't touch nothin' that ain't what we come for."

"Billy, stop being a weenie. Help me get that block."

Billy always gave in to Eric.

They pulled the block toward the well, picked it up, and then heaved it in.

"What's that? D'you hear that, Eric?"

"The block clanking down the well?"

"No, it's somethin' different. It's . . . running."

Eric and Billy turned around and were face-to-face with a raging German Shepherd. Before either of them could shout, they dodged the dog. Eric went left as Billy went right.

Rufus leapt between the two—right into the well.

The boys turned back to the well and peered into its darkness.

A terrible minute passed, then silence.

"I still didn't hear nothin'. That thing must go to China," Eric said.

"Eric, forget about that. What're we going to tell Joe about his dog?"

"The truth. Mostly. You'll figure it out."

The boys sauntered back to Joe's office.

Because their heads were down as they entered, Joe asked, "What's wrong, boys?"

Billy spoke. "Sir, your dog, Rufus. We met him, but he ran after us, over by that well. We were scared, so we ducked, and, well, he jumped into the well!"

Eric and Billy both flinched, uncertain of what Joe's reaction would be.

"Boys, that's impossible. Rufus was tied up to an old engine block. There's no way he could have gotten loose. Now tell me the truth. What happened to my dog?"

This is a fictional story—at least I certainly hope it is. I use it to pose a singular question: what are you chained to that's going to inevitably drag you into a pit?

The specifics of how you answer that question will differ from anyone else reading this book, but unforgiveness often sits at pain's foundation, covered by bitterness, regret, or despair.

Maybe you need to forgive a spouse, a child, or a co-worker. Maybe you need to forgive yourself. Whatever the case, when unforgiveness wraps itself around your heart, you might as well call yourself Rufus and be prepared to involuntarily leap into a pit some near day in the future.

The pit that pain can create is lined with a cesspool of bitterness and emotional poison. Pain's goal is to keep you right where you are in order to slowly destroy your life and the lives of those around you. The pit is created from past hurts and wounds that are still open, stagnant, and toxic. Instead of getting better, we learn to be pain managers.

Once, when I was cleaning up the garage, I tossed a mostly empty butane bottle into the back of my truck. I intended to go by the local hardware store and switch it out for a full bottle the next time I was near the store. But then a month passed.

Every time I'd turn a corner, the butane bottle would topple over and start rolling around in the back of my truck. When I'd get in my truck in the mornings, I'd see that thing back there and hope that today wouldn't be the day it blew up and killed me. The bottle even started altering how I drove. I took corners more slowly, stopped slowly, and was always looking in the back to see if it was OK. Man, it got *stressful*. Every time that thing fell over and slammed up against the cab, I'd cringe.

As I was driving home one day, I had to make a quick turn. *Bam!* That thing fell over again and slammed up against the cab of my truck. Under my breath I said, "Lord, that thing makes me nervous."

Then God spoke to me an incredible, divine word of wisdom in the form of a rhetorical question: "Why don't you take that thing out?"

I realized that instead of getting rid of what could kill me, I had chosen to adapt to it. It had changed the way I drove and had even affected my attitude. I was stressed out all the time.

Lesson learned, God.

We've all been wounded, cut, or hurt in some way during our lives. The problem is that we're driving around *still* wounded and hurt. We haven't allowed ourselves to start healing. We simply try to manage life with the wound still there. Unless we choose to deal with it, our wounds will go from hurt to anger to bitterness, and bitterness turns to death. To be blunt, choosing to *not* forgive is choosing death, even while you're still alive. It's time to get pain out of your life.

Because of the way I treated my body when I was younger, I have scars all over my body. Each scar is a reminder of something that happened in my past. Each mark has its own story.

But none of the scars require my attention any longer.

If you have a wound, you must change the bandage often, being mindful of not hurting it further. Understand that you will be somewhat handicapped in movement until it heals. A wound requires a lot of attention. We must get to the place where our wounds are healing and scars are being formed.

I once heard a pastor talk about forgiveness who said it is our mandatory requirement to forgive and forget all offenses against us. Well, I've searched the Bible and I cannot find a single reference that would command us to *forget* what has happened. Unless you have amnesia or a traumatic experience has stolen your memory, you will likely *never* forget what happened to you.

I've heard other well-intentioned counselors say, "You will get over this. Trust me. It's really not a big deal in the long run of life." While I hope that you do get over your hurt, I don't think minimizing the situation is the right method. Forgiveness is such a big deal that God crucified His Son so we could actually forgive too. So, let's just admit that forgiveness is a big deal and that you will never forget your hurt.

But you can get over it.

You *always* have a choice to become bitter or get better. Don't let your past dictate your future. You always have a choice to dwell in the past or face the present. You always have the choice to forgive. But God knows how hard enacting forgiveness can be—again, forgiveness cost him his Son.

Forgiveness is not an emotion or a feeling. Forgiveness is a choice. At times it is a daily choice, if not an hourly decision. Forgiveness is certainly not a one-time choice. You may choose to forgive, then within days, hours, or even minutes after that, you'll be upset again.

Remember: you have an enemy, and he is not flesh-and-blood. If you can pinch it and it squeals, it's not your enemy. As often as you'll let him, Satan wants to remind you about what happened to you, what you did wrong, or what wrong was done to you.

I have found the following five-step process to be very effective in my battle against un-forgiveness. As soon as I sense myself getting upset, I pray:

1. "Lord, I forgive them."

2. "Lord, I forgive myself for the role I played in the situation."

3. "Lord, I remove myself as judge over them."

4. "Lord, I pray for them and ask that you bless them."

5. "Lord, I resist these thoughts that the enemy is giving me and I turn to You."

Forgiving others is *not* an emotion. Actually, you don't even have to want to forgive someone. You can make the choice to say the words, even when you don't feel like it.

Forgiveness isn't dependent upon whether the offender is remorseful or not either. Most of the people I have had to forgive in my life have never asked for forgiveness. They may not even regret their actions.

Forgiving someone is much more about your health than it is his or her release. You feel wronged and are angry about what took place. Your natural desire is to want to punish them and make them feel hurt for what they have done. But, you don't see them being punished, so you get even angrier. Still, they will go on with their lives even as you destroy yours through anger or bitterness. Forgiving them releases the anger off of you and gives the entire package to God. You are saying, "God, I release this from me and I hand it to You."

Forgive yourself. Stop beating yourself up if you have wronged someone or have brought anything on yourself. If you still find yourself needing to punish yourself when you mess up, or maybe you have a tendency to be glad when others are punished, you may be dealing with a need to forgive yourself. When we feel that we should be punished, we're essentially saying, "What Jesus did on the cross isn't enough for me. I need to be punished again." I know actions have consequences, but you can stop living in your past failures and move toward your future successes.

Removing yourself as judge does not excuse the other person from their actions. It simply allows God to be the rightful judge and removes that burden from you. It isn't your responsibility to have to be judge, jury, executioner, *and* doctor of your healing process all at the same time. Let God be judge. You? Let it go and begin to heal.

Praying for them is, again, not an emotional feeling or desire. Prayer is simply moving away from judging to blessing. When we choose to bless, we line up with God and stop the concert of hatred with the devil.

Lastly, resisting these thoughts will help you put them to bed. "Therefore submit to God. Resist the devil and he will flee from you" (James 4:7, NKJV).

If you can practice this prayer, you will begin to win the battle in your mind. You will experience your anger, rage, and hurt begin to fade. You may have to pray this prayer fifteen times a day, then five times a week, and then two to three times a month, but slowly your anger and unforgiveness will disappear.

9

HERE'S
THE DEAL

When you're on the front side of pain, the hurt seems insurmountable. *How can I get through this? How will I ever get to the other side of this storm?* You *will* get through it as long as you keep your focus on the One who can get you through it.

Whatever you do, you *cannot* ignore unforgiveness. You must **DEAL** with the pain:

Don't get distracted.

Eliminate fear.

Acknowledge Jesus.

Look forward.

Don't get distracted.

When conflict, pain, or suffering happens to you, all kinds of distractions will attempt to push you off the course of forgiveness. Yet it's vitally important to the process that you attempt to remain resolute and unwavering in your choice to forgive. In the middle of every storm, you must remember your destination.

I'm reminded of Jesus's fascinating—and surely frustrating—nap while the disciples were fearing for their lives:

> Now it happened, on a certain day, that He got into a boat with His disciples. And He said to them, "Let us cross over to the other side of the lake." And they launched out. But as they sailed He fell asleep. And a windstorm came down on the lake, and they were filling with water, and were in jeopardy. And they came to Him and awoke Him, saying, "Master, Master, we are perishing!"
>
> Then He arose and rebuked the wind and the raging of the water. And they ceased, and there was a calm. But He said to them,

"Where is your faith?"

And they were afraid, and marveled, saying to one another, "Who can this be? For He commands even the winds and water, and they obey Him! (Luke 8:22–25).

First, we should come to terms with the fact that storms are an inevitable part of life, and especially if you're a Christian. If you're willing to get into the same boat as Jesus, that boat will surely be rocked by a storm in due time. Whatever Jesus has planned, the devil certainly doesn't want to see that come to fruition. Yet we still seem surprised when storms arrive in our lives.

I liken our surprise to a boxer who jumps into the ring, gets clocked by a left-hand uppercut, then cries to the ref, "He hit me! Can he do that?"

The ref laughs in reply. "Yes, he can. You're in a fight. You're going to get hit."

Whenever you choose to live for something greater than yourself, you will face obstacles. Whenever you choose to help others, you will face difficulty. Whenever you choose to follow God's calling above all else, storms will arise.

But here's the good news: God is greater than any storm the devil may conjure. God *sleeps* through the devil's storms. That's how worried he is about what the devil can accomplish.

Consequently, we shouldn't get distracted by the storm. If even the winds and waters obey him, what have we to fear?

Eliminate fear.

I enjoy offering premarital counseling, but sometimes I fear for these young, naive couples who walk into my office hand-in-hand. In the elongated honeymoon phase that seems to begin from the moment he drops to one knee to ask for her hand in marriage, seldom do problems raise their heads. In counseling, I'm just a hurdle for them to jump so they can get to the wedding day and the actual honeymoon. There's nothing intrinsically wrong with that. The couple is so in love, and maybe so new to that kind of love, that they're essentially living with blinders on. They can't see what they don't want to see about the other person.

But anywhere from one to three years later, those blinders fall off, and the reality of what they've gotten themselves into suddenly comes into stark view. The storms of life and the inevitable collision of two imperfect people living together 24/7 sometimes bring an abrupt end to the honeymoon phase. That's when the real work of a marriage begins. That's when they visit me again, though they're no longer walking in hand-in-hand. They may not even be arriving in the same car anymore.

Once they're in my office, the words they use to describe where they've found themselves are almost universally similar:

"He doesn't care about me like he used to."

"I didn't know it was going to be this hard."

"I don't think we're going to make it."

Essentially, they're doubting their decision. Regret has crept in as reality has set in. Worry and fear have begun driving the relationship. If left unchecked, such fear of, "Will this ever change?" will ensure that the marriage *will* die in divorce much less never change.

In a way, the disciples found themselves in the same boat. They feared for their lives when their decisions to follow Christ met the reality of the world. Like a newly married couple facing their first real relationship crisis, the disciples were in the middle of a journey. They could choose fear or faith.

They chose fear. They chose to believe that something bad was about to happen. Even when a man who had done incredible miracles *physically* resided with them, they gave in to fear. Yet still Jesus saved them.

We could eliminate so much personal and relational heartache if we would just go to Jesus first, in faith, and believe that he will accomplish his goals in our lives. Fear and faith are two sides of the same coin of how we can think about the future. The only difference is the object of that belief. Either you believe the world has more power than God or God has more power than the world.

Before their tumultuous trip, Jesus had told the disciples that they were going to cross to the other side of the lake. He didn't warn them about the storm, though as fisherman they likely knew of the possibility. He didn't speak calming words to them when the storm came.

Rather, he eliminated their source of fear in the middle of their journey because he said, "We're going to the other side."

If they'd just believed him from the outset, they wouldn't have feared for their lives when the going got rough.

Acknowledge Jesus.

Believe with all your being that Jesus is with you even in the midst of a raging storm. He may be silent, or, as in the case of the disciples on the boat, he may be asleep, but if he's *with* you, you already have everything you need to endure the storm.

The harder truth to accept is that sometimes Jesus will allow you to suffer through an entire storm. But you can still have peace and full faith in God during those moments because he holds all power. He is the peace that passes all understanding, even when the world around you seems like it's going to give way at any moment.

Remember, Peter got out of the boat and walked *on top of the water.* The wind and waves did not decrease. In fact, Jesus sat back and watched the disciples sail right into the storm. When Peter got out of the boat, he stayed above the storm as long as his eyes were on Jesus. When Peter placed his gaze on the stormy sea, he sank. I guess Jesus would later nickname him The Rock for a reason.

Rather than allowing yourself to fall prey to the Enemy's repeated attempts to make you doubt God's goodness and greatness ("Did God really say, 'You must not eat from any tree in the garden'?" (Genesis 3:1b)), believe that the one who created all is more powerful than the slithering one who was made.

Jesus never panics. He's not afraid of what the future holds, and neither is he surprised when misfortunate befalls you. But he weeps along with you, as he did for Mary and Martha in their loss of Lazarus, even though Jesus knew he was going to resurrect the man. He cares deeply for you, as a mother hen does her chicks. He longs to be your source of hope.

Trust him in the storms. Remember the goodness he's shown you in the past and believe on the goodness he will show you once you've reached the other side. Place your faith in his power, which is strong enough to calm even the most tumultuous of seas.

Look forward.

In one of the most heart-wrenching scenes of the Old Testament, King David's son dies as a result of David's sinful ways. As a reminder, David had committed adultery with a married woman in his kingdom, and to make matters infinitely worse, he used his power as king to have the woman's husband placed on the front lines of battle so that he would be killed. Following the prophet

Nathan's rebuke of King David for his sins, 1 Samuel 12:15–23 recounts the events of that terrible night:

After Nathan had gone home, the Lord struck the child that Uriah's wife had borne to David, and he became ill. David pleaded with God for the child. He fasted and spent the nights lying in sackcloth on the ground. The elders of his household stood beside him to get him up from the ground, but he refused, and he would not eat any food with them.

On the seventh day the child died. David's attendants were afraid to tell him that the child was dead, for they thought, "While the child was still living, he wouldn't listen to us when we spoke to him. How can we now tell him the child is dead? He may do something desperate."

David noticed that his attendants were whispering among themselves, and he realized the child was dead. "Is the child dead?" he asked.

"Yes," they replied, "he is dead."

Then David got up from the ground. After he had washed, put on lotions and changed his clothes, he went into the house of the Lord and worshiped. Then he went to his own house, and at his request they served him food, and he ate.

His attendants asked him, "Why are you acting this way? While the child was alive, you fasted and wept, but now that the child is dead, you get up and eat!"

He answered, "While the child was still alive, I fasted and wept. I thought, 'Who knows? The Lord may be gracious to me and let the child live.' But now that he is dead, why should I go on fasting? Can I bring him back again? I will go to him, but he will not return to me."

David's actions following the death of his son seem callous at best. Even his attendants noticed: "Why are you acting this way?" You can almost hear the shock in their voices.

Despite his many flaws, David was still a wise man chosen by God to both lead his people and to be part of Jesus's lineage. As evidenced by his reply to his attendants, David knew there was nothing he could do to fix his past. His son was gone and would not return, and David knew his son had paid the ultimate price for his own grievous sins. David could have lived in regret and mourned his loss for the rest of his days, and most people then as now would not have faulted him for that. But David also realized that he could only look forward to what lay ahead of him, to learn what he could from his terrible mistakes, and to move into the life and leadership that God desired of him.

We must not be afraid to face present pain, to let others know that we may be suffering, or to ardently pray for ourselves when the struggles of life threaten to drown us. But neither should we allow that pain to suffocate us for the rest of our lives. We shouldn't live with even one foot in the past, especially when that foot might be cemented into a painful experience. As Martin Luther King, Jr. said, who suffered much during his too-brief life, "If you can't fly then run, if you can't run then walk, if you can't walk then crawl, but whatever you do you have to keep moving forward."

I was once asked to perform a wedding at a very nice ranch resort in Colorado, which had a lot of fun and exciting things to do. One activity was a ropes and climbing course where anyone could ascend to the top of a very high tower.

I watched as fourteen-year-old Carter began his climb. He scaled the base with no problem. He climbed the fifteen-foot ladder effortlessly. Then, as he jumped into the air, he caught a rope and climbed to the next stage. Now at over thirty feet in the air, Carter jumped *again* to reach the next level. But his hands slipped and he fell. Fortunately, Carter was attached to a safety harness and was gently lowered back down to the ground, where he landed on his feet, unharmed.

His younger brother Maddox had watched his brother's entire climb—and fall. Nervous but undaunted, Maddox was slow and cautious as he began his climb. He couldn't move like his brother, but I was still amazed that a *seven-year-old* would even try something like that climb.

As he climbed the fifteen-foot ladder, Maddox froze about three steps from the next ladder.

His father and older brother encouraged him. "Just take one step at a time Maddox!"

When he did, they cheered like crazy.

"Don't look down, Maddox! Look up!"

He took another step.

"Don't look back, Maddox! Look forward and take another step!"

Another step.

"Great job, son! You got this! You can do this! I know you're scared, but you can do it, Maddox. We're right here for you."

Every step got Maddox closer to the top of that ladder. I was spellbound watching this seven-year-old stand twenty feet in the air. He prepared himself for the next level.

"Reach for the rope, Maddox. You can do it!"

But the rope line was out of his reach.

And just like he'd seen his brother do, Maddox jumped.

Everyone watching sucked in every molecule of air in that moment. I'm fairly certain the wildlife stopped their racket too. For a brief second, the world paused as Maddox glided toward the rope just out of his reach.

But he missed.

He fell.

To deafening applause and cheers, Maddox was gently lowered to the ground.

Maddox had gone further than he thought he could because of the cheers of his family. His family cheered him on with confidence because they all knew that he would be caught and lowered safely to the ground. How did they know? Because they'd already been through the trials of the course and knew how it would end, no matter the climb's success or failure. They had all fallen as well, and they had all been saved.

When you get over your fear and through your trial, you can look back and cheer someone else through the same storm. Help them find their way. Be their safety harness and cheering audience.

God longs to use our past trials to shape our character and have us ready to help others. God doesn't waste any of your pain. What the enemy meant for evil, God can and will use for good. If you let him, God will use your journey to reach back and guide someone else through what you've just survived.

When I get on an airplane, I don't want a pilot who's never experienced a thunderstorm or flown in icy conditions. I want a pilot who's weathered many storms and knows how to navigate through them if and when they arise. You don't really know that you can get through a storm until you do. Then you know for sure that you can get others through.

Remember, when facing pain, DEAL with it:

- **D**on't get distracted.

- **E**liminate fear.

- **A**cknowledge God.

- **L**ook forward.

And you will get to the other side. I promise.
Even better, God promises.

10

THERE YOU ARE

"Are you Jeff Burandt?"

"Yes, officer. I am. What's going on?"

As Jeff stood with his front door open, his mind raced to grab hold of any reason the cop was there before the officer could say his next words. Jeff mentally checked off his family members: *The girls are upstairs in their room. Lisa's making dinner. Chris walked down the block a few hours ago to hang out with friends. What is this—*

"Is Chris Burandt your son?"

"Yes, officer. He is. *What's going on?*"

The normally stoic officer took a step back at the anger and fear hiding just beneath the surface of Jeff's question.

"We believe your son was in an accident. He was hit by a car a few hours ago. He's at the hospital now, but you and your wife need to get there as soon as you can."

In that moment, the wave goodbye that his fifteen-year-old son had just given him a short time ago flashed into Jeff's mind.

Jeff didn't reply to the officer, but yelled down the hallway for his wife.

When they arrived at the hospital, they found Chris unconscious.

My wife and I, as well as others who deeply cared for the Burandts, got to the hospital as soon as we could. We prayed. We comforted. We sat in silence. We wondered why.

The infinite hours of that first day turned into weeks. After a month had passed, it seemed like Chris had been getting better, but he suddenly passed from this life to heaven. In short order, just a month after their son had suffered an unimaginable accident, Jeff and Lisa found themselves doing the unthinkable: choosing a casket in which to lay their fifteen-year-old son's lifeless body to rest.

Soon after, I walked through a field with Jeff as we chose a cemetery plot in which to lay his son. In those quiet moments, I thought what every parent would think: how unfair and premature for a parent to have to bury a child. The pain that they were enduring seemed unendurable to me. But somehow in the midst of the chaos, Jeff and Lisa knew God was near. They felt his peace despite the storm that threatened to overtake them.

The funeral produced one of the biggest turnouts we had ever seen in our church. As I prepared to speak at the funeral, I felt God encouraging me to say what Chris would say if he'd had the opportunity. In the presence of close to one thousand of his grieving friends and family, I said:

> If Chris could be with us today, that charismatic, guitar-playing fifteen-year-old with a smile that could light up any room, I think this is what he'd want each of you to know: there is a heaven and there is a hell. I want you to believe that Jesus Christ is everything he claims to be. He is as real as you and I are. I ask you to give your life to him and trust him. He loves you so much that he gave his Son for you so that you can live here with me in heaven for all eternity.

I asked those in attendance to pray with me, and then I gave an invitation for anyone to ask Jesus into their lives and trust him for salvation. Forty-two people raised their hands at that funeral to signify that their lives had been irrevocably changed in that moment. They'd heard what Chris would have told them, prayed the sinner's prayer of repentance, and become new followers of God.

During the month of Chris's recovery, I often thought, "Where are you, God?"

In those life-altering moments at his funeral, I thought, "There you are."

Did God cause the accident that took Chris's life? Absolutely not. But did God transform that pain for his glory and the good of others? Absolutely. God doesn't waste heartache, tears, or trials when we lay our sorrows at the feet of the Man of Sorrows. Remember, "He was despised and forsaken of men, A man of sorrows and *acquainted with grief*" (Isaiah 53:3a, NASB).

My favorite image of Dana Finch, a beloved wife, high-energy teacher, mom to three boys, and foster parent to nine kids, has to be her sitting on a recliner in the back of a pickup, reading a good book and waiting for her sons to finish bird-hunting. She'd told her sons that if she was going, they'd have to load the recliner onto the truck.

Her son Luke recalls his mom's singular ways of encouragement. In high school, he played baseball, but never started a game. The coach had a cooler in the dugout emblazoned with the words, "FOR STARTERS ONLY." When Dana heard about this, she bought a bigger cooler and stocked it with Gatorade and water. Her cooler read, "FOR NON-STARTERS ONLY. IT TAKES EVERYONE TO MAKE A TEAM." Dana was the kind of mom every kid would have loved to have.

She was also involved in a number of activities outside of her teaching job and prized role as wife and mother. She volunteered at numerous local agencies, taught a Bible study at her church, and hosted a TV show every Tuesday called "Connect and Communicate." She followed her entrepreneurial leanings too, and traveled throughout the U.S. and Canada to teach and consult with educators through her own business, Principle Impact Strategies. In other words, she was generous with her time and talents, and there's no doubt that she impacted hundreds, if not thousands, of students, teachers, friends, and family through her work.

So it made very little sense when her energy began to ebb while she was working as an interim headmaster at a local Christian academy. She was always overflowing with seemingly boundless energy to do all she desired to do. When that energy level significantly dropped, she underwent a thorough medical checkup. The results were devastating: pancreatic cancer. Over the few months following her diagnosis, she and her family learned of its severity.

During what many people would have rightfully thought was the end of their life, the indomitable spirit of Dana Finch chose to honor God despite her increasing pain. She opted to use her situation as a platform to encourage others who were suffering like her.

Dana blogged about her entire ordeal, providing doctors' reports, testimonies, and scripture, and detailing how her family was dealing with her decline. Her encouraging testimonies were read by over 92,000 viewers from as far away as Japan, Turkey, and Istanbul.

Fifteen months after her diagnosis, Dana was down to eighty-three pounds and struggling to catch her breath. Still, she didn't let that stop her from climbing onto her stool at her church to teach her Bible study. A few days after one such study, Dana suffered a stroke and God called her home at the age of forty-nine.

When I learned of her diagnosis, I asked, "Where are you, God?"

When I heard of her passing, I asked, "Where are you, God?"

When I thought about the husband and children she left behind, I asked, "Where are you, God?"

My wife and I, along with *three thousand others*, attended Dana's funeral. Each of her sons spoke about their mom, some seriously and some hilariously. Tears of sorrow and laughter freely mixed on the faces of all in attendance in maybe the truest visualization of "bittersweet" I've ever seen. Each of the boys ended their remembrances by reciting Proverbs 31:27–28: "She watches over the ways of her household, And does not eat the bread of idleness. Her children rise up and call her blessed." What an incredibly appropriate verse for Dana Finch, whom no one would have dared called "idle," and whose sons obviously and proudly called her blessed.

Dana's husband, Scott, then spoke his own remembrances. He praised her as his wife and told us what an honor it had been for him to make a life with her, and even to suffer alongside her during those last few and utterly trying months. He ended by quoting Proverbs 31:28–30: "Her husband also praises her: 'Many daughters have done well, But you excel them all.' Charm is deceitful and beauty is passing, But a woman who fears the Lord, she shall be praised." Again, the words written ages ago seemed a perfect fit for a woman who was taken far too soon.

During her funeral, I had the same thoughts as I'd had during fifteen-year-old Chris Burandt's. Why would God take the life of someone who was doing so much good for his kingdom? Why does an accident on an otherwise normal day, or a diagnosis of a deadly disease, have to usher death into families who seek to honor God? Why aren't we given easy answers to the questions of pain and sorrow and death and tragedy this side of heaven?

My questions weren't answered in that moment. As this short book witnesses, I'm still grappling with the problem of pain, just as so many other authors and pastors have done so for centuries. But we're offered hints as to why we must endure pain this side of heaven.

After Dana's sons and her husband had spoken at her funeral, every one of the three thousand people in attendance spontaneously stood to their feet and gave a standing ovation—a strange occurrence at a funeral, to be sure. I don't believe the ovation was for Dana, as much as she certainly deserved it, but rather for God's glory having been revealed both in her life and in her death.

In that moment, I remember thinking, "There you are, God!"

———————

I share those two hard stories of death because death is the ultimate form of suffering that the living must endure. To lose someone close to you is to lose part of you. Such grief may lessen with time, but you will certainly be marked by that person's absence for the rest of your life. And I've been in ministry long enough to know that the problem of pain and death has prevented many people from believing in God because they blame him for taking their loved one away.

While there are no easy answers as to why we must suffer the pain of losing a loved one, there is a clear pathway that's been marked for you when you lose someone, or when suffering personally afflicts you: don't run away from God. Rather, run to him.

Brother Lawrence, a seventeenth-century monk known for writing *The Practice of the Presence of God*, says this much better than I could:

> Instead of always asking God for deliverance from your pain, out of love for Him ask for His strength to resolutely bear all that He allows you to go through. Such prayers are hard at first, but very pleasing to God and become sweet to those that love Him. Love sweetens pain and when one loves God one suffers for His sake and with joy and courage. Do so I beseech you. Comfort yourself with Him. He is the only physician for all our illnesses. He is the father of the afflicted and always ready to help. Seek no consolation elsewhere . . . . Take courage and pray to Him for strength to

endure. Above all get in the habit of thinking of God often and forget Him the least you can. If we were all accustomed to the practice of His presence, of God, discomfort would be greatly alleviated. How can we pray to Him without being with Him? How can we be with Him but in thinking of Him often? How can we think of Him often but by a holy habit, which we should form of it? I use no other method to endure this world and I advise all the world to do the same.

In other words, if you're in pain, seek the help of the Great Doctor.

I have pondered the pain in my past and have wondered how I endured it. I remember literally just trying to breathe. I know what a panic attack feels like. I have woken up in the morning, wishing the pain was a nightmare, but quickly realized it was all too real. Nothing was going to save me from that circumstance. The pain existed and I was right in the middle of it.

The rising anger, the grieving ache in my spirit, the confusion and fear that would come rushing in—it was all paralyzing. I couldn't turn my brain off. My mind ran at the speed of light. The pain was out of my control and overtaking me.

My brain could ask a hundred questions a minute with no answers in sight: *Why did this happen? How will I survive? Am I going to lose everything? Is this really happening? God, where are you? What can I do to stop this? What is going to happen to my family?*

Every breath was intentional. "Breathe, David. Just keep breathing."

Every step was intentional. "Just get up and walk with one foot in front of the other."

I know what it feels like to live your life in one-to-five-minute increments throughout the day: devastating. But I endured it and am better and stronger for it.

You will be better and stronger as you go to God and trust him to carry you.

If you're hurting right now, don't give in to bitterness toward others or toward God. Hidden bitterness hardens your heart and creates an abscess that will poison you. When you hold onto such bitterness—when you're angry with God about what you think he should have done—you're agreeing with the Evil One's very first lie, "Did

God really say . . . ?" That's a sure path to experiencing more pain.

Rather, allow the light of God's truth to shatter your bitterness so that you might become better. Hold on to God's unchanging hand and watch him set you free from the enemy's chains. Have faith to believe that he sees you even when you can't see him. Tell a trusted friend how you really feel in the midst of your pain.

Tell God how you feel. He knows already, but sometimes I think he wants us to know what we really feel, and prayer is the safest place for him to gently guide you toward wholeness. If you need words, try these:

"Lord, I know you didn't cause this, and I know you don't get joy out of my pain, but I'm here and I'm deeply hurting. I don't know what to do with this, and I wish it would just go away, but I'm bringing my pain to you. I lay it at your feet and I cry out to you for help."

You may not be given an immediate response, but pray again, cry before him, cry out to him. As you do this with the community that God will bring you, you will see one step turn into two, one hour of sleep will turn into four, day by day you will get stronger and you will know that God is there. In time someone may come into your life who's been suffering the same pain. Or, someone who doesn't know God may need to hear your story about how God brought you through the darkest time of your life.

If we could trust God that he knows what's best, even when we're suffering, I believe we'll witness and experience the depth of love and care he has for those who hurt. Remember, remember, remember: "The Lord is near to the brokenhearted And saves those who are crushed in spirit" (Psalm 34:18, NASB).

A day is coming when we will dwell in a land of no tears, no pain, no sorrow, and no death. But until that day comes, let Christ come to you, comfort you, lead you, guide you, and set you free from the chains of the enemy. Work toward being stronger and better by his grace.

You *will* get through this.

Though today you may be asking, "Where are you, God?" I promise that one day, if you'll run to him and accept his help, he'll make himself known in your life. Then you'll exclaim just like I did, "There you are, God. There you are!"

ABOUT THE AUTHOR

David Vestal has more than twenty-five years of experience developing life-coaching and discipleship skills. He is the founding pastor of Lighthouse Christian Fellowship Church and president of Daybreak Ministries.

A dynamic and gifted communicator, David has been a public speaker to address conferences, organizations, leaders, companies, churches, and staff for a wide range of topics including leadership, culture, growth, vision, and how to thrive in your God-given gifts and talents.

Read more at www.davidvestal.org
or connect with David on Twitter at
twitter.com/davidvestal.

Made in the USA
Charleston, SC
27 January 2017